THE WORLD OF ISLAM

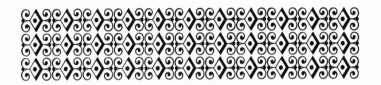

The World of Islam

(LE MONDE ISLAMIQUE: ESSAI DE GÉOGRAPHIE RELIGIEUSE)

By Xavier de Planhol

RXTSA

CORNELL UNIVERSITY PRESS

Ithaca and London

CORNELL UNIVERSITY PRESS

English translation first published 1959
Second printing 1967
Third printing 1970

International Standard Book Number 0-8014-9830-9

PRINTED IN THE UNITED STATES OF AMERICA
BY VALLEY OFFSET, INC.

Introduction

THE geography of religion is a recent subject of study. To be sure, many distinguished men have been interested in the mutual relations of geography and religion ever since the great voyages brought Europeans into closer and closer contact with foreign religions and strange customs. But the problem is extraordinarily complex. When the relations seem obvious between a material phenomenon (an aspect of the countryside or a way of using the soil, for example) and certain elements of spiritual order, is it a question of certain abstract conceptions involving practical consequences, or, alternately, have everyday practical necessities somehow undergone a projection into the religious sphere? Did certain heretics take refuge in the mountains and develop there a new way of life because they were heretics, or did they become heretics and remain such because they were mountain dwellers, living their own lives outside the great currents of thought? The answer to this question is often doubtful, and sometimes impossible, to the extent that the observer declines to indulge in one sort of a priori scheme or another. Between the ruthless simplicity of determinism and the shamefaced admission of impotence there remains only a narrow path for the reasoned approach.

This explains why serious studies in this field have hitherto been restricted, of necessity, to the mere collection of facts. (An exception must be made for works of religious sociology which are multiplying in western Europe—in France one notes particularly the work of G. Le Bras—but these are set up on a somewhat different basis.) Thus the fine treatise on general religious geography by P. Deffontaines [1] provides a great deal of documentation for very different theories. The little book that follows has no other aim than to exhibit the state of the record with regard to one of the great monotheistic religions of the world. With respect to this religion particularly, its location in a specific biological-geographical zone is very plain, and its relations with the material substratum of life are very evident. The book envisages a double audience, of students of Islam and geographers. To the first group, from whose works the author has drawn freely, he would recall the importance of these fundamental concerns and the interest which would often be derived from taking them more

---

[1] *Géographie et religions* (Paris, 1948). See also by the same author "Valeur et limites de l'explication religieuse en géographie humaine," *Diogène*, No. 2 (1953), 64–79.

fully into account.[2] For the geographers, he seeks to establish, as a preliminary to all further study of human geography in the Moslem countries, the basic facts which will permit them to distinguish not only the role of geographical influences in the spread of Islam and its different shadings but the part played by religious factors in determining the actual physical features of Islamic countries. Finally, this book may help the general public to become aware of Islam's place in the world and to understand various external aspects of the culture which reveal themselves often even to the hastiest inspection.

As for the fundamental problems indicated above, the author makes no pretense of offering any wholesale solutions to them. At best, putting down the first principles may allow us to pick out the important details and assess the full complexity of the interacting processes. Here as elsewhere only long and patient researches into the history of particular regions will yield the light of certainty. Still we must deal with this most indispensable of all the objectives of geographical analysis. If only to eliminate them from the account, we must undertake to determine the place of religious and psychological factors in the utilization of the soil. This is a necessary preliminary to any scientific study of "man the cultivator," a prerequisite to any rational estimate of man's place on the

[2] Cf. on this subject the justified complaints of C. Cahen, "L'histoire économique et sociale de l'Islam," *Studia islamica*, III (1955), 93–116, and those of R. Brunschvig, *ibid.*, I (1953), 7–8. See also S. D. Goitein, "The Rise of the Near-Eastern Bourgeoisie in Early Islamic Times," *Journal of World History*, III (1957), 583–604.

planet. The author will be content if this little book, if only by its inadequacies and the criticisms that it provokes, serves to focus attention on the need for further studies.

Since the character of this work precludes all detailed critical apparatus, nearly all the references have been kept apart from the text, and the reader is referred for further information on sources to the general bibliography at the end of the volume. The author does not, however, wish to overlook his obligations in a vast area where the role of personal experience is necessarily limited. As for the problem of transcribing names from foreign tongues, the author has decided, upon mature reflection, to avoid all rigid systems, since his work is intended primarily for a general, unprofessional audience. He has simply tried to come as close as possible to current usage, whether it is good or bad.

Introduction
to the English Edition

IN the English edition certain obvious errors of the French text (Paris, 1957) have been corrected, and additions and revisions have been made to bring the bibliography up to date. We have also modified slightly certain over-all judgments and taken account of the general ideas regarding our book that have appeared in the valuable reviews of A. Allix in the *Revue de géographie de Lyon*, 1958, 79–80 (valuable especially in regard to the Islamic faith as a geographical agent) and in those of J. Despois in the *Annales de géographie*, May–June 1958 (in regard to the role of the "route to the Indies" and of navigation in the expansion of Islam).

X. DE P.

July 1958

Contents

THE WORLD OF ISLAM

CHAPTER I

The Geographical Mark of Islam

ISLAM AND THE CITY

THE mark of Islam has been impressed on the life and appearance of its cities more indelibly than anywhere else. There is a special look to an Islamic city, composed of a tangle of blocks badly ventilated by a labyrinth of twisted alleys and dark courts, the low houses endlessly broken up along their little courtyards. There is also a special feeling about an Islamic city, dominated by a contrast between the noisy bazaar and the silence of the residential districts, where one hears only the cries and games of the children. Nowhere perhaps can one feel this more vividly than in the area of the Aegean Sea, where Anatolian Islam is only a few miles distant from the Greek islands, which are Christian. The setting of the cities is often similar, the houses themselves are often identical (a goodly number of the Anatolian coastal towns were built by the Greeks before the transfer of populations); and yet, though the Aegean ports are among the most animated of the Turkish towns, a trip to the Greek islands is like an orgy of light and noise.

General Conditions of Islamic Urban Life

The growth of cities. These basic facts take on particular importance in view of the large number of cities established in Islamic countries. We shall see shortly that there are deep-seated reasons for this exceptional proliferation, but at present let us be content with the fact itself. In countries which until recently have been quite untouched by the industrial revolution and where the instability of agriculture and the preponderance of nomadic tribes in the vast empty spaces of the deserts have rendered precarious the very basis of regional life, it is certainly paradoxical to see that Islam has been able to multiply cities almost at will. The functions of acting as storehouses and of organizing caravans to the outskirts of the Mediterranean and of the desert, operations which have been incidental to the intermediary role played by Near Eastern countries in world trade up to modern times—these have certainly helped to form and support the cities of Islam.

But many of these creations seem to be specifically the products of Islam itself. The founding of a city, an arbitrary act of creation *ex nihilo*, is particularly frequent in these regions. Such behavior may seem paradoxical in people professing a religion propagated by nomadic Arabs. And certainly the nomad always mistrusts cities. The action of creating a town, a *tamsir*, offends his whole way of thinking. The first towns of the nomads who left Arabia were often nothing but semipermanent camps placed at the edge of the steppe or the desert for the use of armies too remote from their base of supplies to return every year to Arabia. They were loosely organized settlements, provisional and unfortified, out of which one could easily slip into the freedom of the open steppe, and which in fact only became cities subsequently. But these city camps (sometimes called *fostats* from the Latin *fossatum* by way of the late Greek *fossaton*, "camp"), these military patchworks created alongside a pre-Islamic settlement to supply the needs of war, seem like an affirmation of the Islamic personality itself. (They were particularly numerous in the region of the Mesopotamian boundary line but are found everywhere; of this type are Basra, Kufa, Hira, Jabiya in Transjordan, the original Fostat [Old Cairo], which grew up next to the so-called pre-Islamic Babylon, Kairawan, for a long time the capital of Tunisia, and Tagrart [a Berber word meaning "camp"], the future Tlemcen in North Africa.) These settlements affirmed the originality of the Moslem city vis-à-vis the past at the same time that they represented an expression of a general movement to settle down—a movement which existed before Islam and is not particularly in question here. From this same sort of urban creation grew the ribats, a variety of fortified barracks used to house soldiers in the holy war and also as monasteries in which communities were assembled under the direction of religious chiefs. Islam scattered these ribats the length of its frontiers, where they often became the seeds of

very important cities. This took place on the eastern
flank of the Maghreb (Sousse, Sfax, Monastir, Tripoli),
where ribats served to mount an offensive against Sicily.
They are also found on the Atlantic coast of Africa,
where they served as defenses against the Normans, but
are rarer on the north coast. Those in the interior served
primarily as pious retreats, but various towns owe their
existence to ribats, for example, Salé, which was founded
in the vicinity of the heretical Berghawata, and Taza, a
frontier post supporting the Almohad expansion against
the Almoravids who held the plains.

A second class of city creation particularly frequent in
Islamic countries is the princely town. These manifestations of the royal will always served to mark the birth of
dynasties and to affirm their authority. The princes who
had built up the power of a dynasty wished to build also
their own capitals. Holiday towns and princely pleasure
palaces were a natural sequence to political capitals; for
example, Samarra, capital of the Abbassids. Such pleasure
palaces are particularly numerous in Morocco; to them
have been added the creations of the Almohads, the Almoravids, and the Merinids. In what measure is this taste
for new building, often abandoned as casually as it was
built, explained by psychological factors? Men were
often influenced by a superstitious fear of bad luck if they
used buildings raised for earlier dynasties and associated
with the scenes of their death. Perhaps also the marked
inclination of princes to create towns on the outskirts of
already existing cities may be explained by the desire to
avoid the noise and the turbulent, truculent crowds of the
cities. Without denying the previous hypothesis, one

might perhaps add another motive, that of avoiding the scandal which the frivolity of a royal court in the close confines of a city might cast on the rigorous purity of Islamic morals. In any event the princely town is everywhere present.

Finally, it is beyond question that the social role and controlling functions which in primitive Islam marked the middle-class citizens of Hejaz, of Mecca and Taif, exerted a favorable influence on the growth of cities. The citizens of the sacred cities had long since been accustomed to the conduct of business, and their economic ambitions were scarcely conceivable outside the framework of a city. The establishment of hostels for the nomads, which quickly turned into urban centers, is one of the most obvious factors in the extension of Islam.

The Islamic ideal and the life of cities. But the essential fact is that Islam has need of the city to realize its social and religious ideals. The religion encourages the *tamsir*, the founding of a town. The establishment of a town is a highly laudable act, and innumerable pious legends are attached to town origins. Certain blessings have always been associated with a stay at Medina; a special dispensation was necessary to leave it. Conversely the most meritorious of acts is the *hijra*, or hegira, the departure for Medina, and thus the migration toward the city. Nomads, on the other hand (and in the countries where Islam originally took shape there were almost no social classes other than nomads and city dwellers), never have any function for Islam save that of second-class recruits. In armed conflicts they are often indispensable auxiliaries—as warriors they are thoroughly advantageous—but outside the profession of arms they are often thought to be bad men and dubious religionists, brawlers and blasphemers. A celebrated prescript warns against milk in these terms: "What I dread for my people is milk, where the devil crouches between the foam and the cream. They will drink of the milk, and then return to the desert, leaving behind the centers where men pray together." Elsewhere the Koran says, "The Arabs of the desert are the most hardened in their impiety and hypocrisy" (IX, 98).

What now are the reasons for this disapproval? First of all, the cornerstone of Islam is prayer, and communal prayer. The most important prayer of all occurs on Friday, when the whole community assembles to pray. Such a custom requires a permanent mosque, where an important assembly like this can take place. Originally the city was simply the place of the great Friday-prayer mosque, as opposed to the several little mosques for daily prayer, which were more precarious and mobile edifices. Various discussions have taken place among theologians concerning the precise places where the Friday prayer may be made, and the reason for them is simply a rigorous definition of what a city is. The dispute usually concerns the importance of settlements which we might call towns, or little cities, or big villages, and the question is which of them deserve the honor of being cities. In every case it is the exclusive privilege of settled folk. The mosque must be permanent, and it must be completely built. Certain strict writers hold that a Friday prayer is of no effect if it is made in a chapel which has been left open to the sky by a hole in the ceiling, even a temporary one. Even aside from the Friday prayer, the rhythm of Islamic religious practices is made for city dwellers. The mosque with its basin for sacred ablutions, and the elaborate installation which that requires, the five daily prayers at the call of the muezzin, the fast of Ramadan with its nocturnal activities—these are town rather than country practices.

In the second place, city life, which is indispensable to communal prayer, is equally indispensable to the dignity of life which Islam demands. The true Moslem must lead a middle-class life. Women must be veiled, a requirement difficult to reconcile with the circumstances of nomad existence and troublesome even under the conditions of rural life. This rigorous and prudish ideal is that of the ascetic merchants of Hejaz. Here again Islam seeks the security of the city rather than the freedom of the open fields. By virtue of its social constraints as well as its spiritual demands Islam is a city religion. The city is a military fortress, but, more importantly, it is a pillar of the faith and a framework within which to live the good life.

The lack of municipal life. And yet these Islamic cities are strangely lacking in cohesion. This is the fundamental difference which separates them as much from the cities of antiquity as from the medieval cities of Europe. The Roman city rested at the center of a territory which belonged to the city; the medieval town in the western world was a refuge, usually cut off from the neighboring countryside. In both cases there were a lively feeling of solidarity, a notable pride in the city, and many close forms of understanding and co-operation among the citizens. There is nothing of the sort in an Islamic city. It has no separate municipal life. No privilege of exception, no special freedom of action, attaches to citizenship. The

price paid for the predominance of religious conceptions
in Islamic social organization is the absence of any political interest in the community as such. Nothing intervenes
to temper the absolutism of the prince, whose power is
the expression of divine might itself, unless it is the moderating but often limited influence of the representative
of the faith. In North Africa the assemblies and democratic councils of the Berbers have sometimes managed to
survive, but they have been able to play an active role
only insofar as the princely power has been weakened. In
the face of this arbitrary power from which nothing pro-
tects him, the Moslem conceals his private life and that
of his family, so far as he can, behind the forbidding walls
of his house, in the maze of alleys and back streets which
half seal off his residential district. Although a scholar
(C. Cahen) has recently modified a bit the extreme state-
ments that deny all municipal life whatever in every
Islamic country (there are traces of it in the Orient before
the Mongols), the fact still remains that there is no sign
of it in the structure of the cities. The municipal official is
the *muhtasib*, who has charge of nothing more than the
police and the surveillance of the markets and bazaars,
which are the chief manifestations of community life on
the nonreligious level. But there is no supervision of municipal growth or planning. A capital like Istanbul had to
wait till 1855 for its first municipal commission; until then
it was given over to the arbitrary and capricious will of
the janissaries and their private armies, to the administrators of pious foundations, or to the prince's architect in
chief. This state of things had an enormous influence on
the organization and structure of the cities.

Structure and Organization of Moslem Towns

These two facts, the urban ideal implicit in Islamic religion and the absence of municipal organization in Islamic countries, go far toward accounting for the form and appearance of the cities. From the first influence derives the strong, strict framing of the towns, their general appearance of having been established in consequence of rigid principles. From the second influence derives the extraordinary anarchy of detail, which conceals the basic skeleton beneath a proliferation of parasitic features.

General elements of organization. The Moslem town obeys a number of well-defined general rules. These are the concentric arrangement and hierarchical division of the different quarters, topographic partitioning and corporative concentration in commercial districts, and ethnic as well as religious segregation in residential areas.

From the pre-eminence of religious functions in the city derives the central position of the chief mosque. It is the heart of the whole complex, set on the site of the agora or forum in the pre-Islamic towns. In the immediate neighborhood one finds the bazaar, a commercial district, with its booths (*souks*) and rows of shops, generally set up around the khans, or combination hotels and warehouses. In this area too one generally finds the public baths. If the *hammam* (public bathhouse) is foreign in origin, borrowed by Islam as by Sassanid Persia from Mediterranean civilizations, if numerous ethical precepts condemn it, sometimes moderately but often violently, as a place of abomination and scandal where nakedness leads straight to debauchery, its usefulness in keeping oneself clean has earned it a place in Islam and a position, actually, among the central institutions of the town. As for the seat of the government or its representative, the *makhzen* quarter in Morocco and the *ark* of Persian towns, it is generally found not at the center of the city, strictly de- fined, but on the outskirts, ready to defend itself against popular uprisings. The Jewish quarter also, in order to preserve itself against mob violence, generally locates it- self in the immediate vicinity of the palace (see, for ex- ample, the *mellahs*, or ghettos, of Fez, Tlemcen, and Constantine). Bordering on these public quarters are the residential districts, with their network of main streets oriented usually toward the bazaar, especially in medium- sized or small cities. Then come the semirural districts, urban in appearance but occupied by farm workers, and then the district of the cemeteries. Islamic burying grounds contrast sharply with the church-oriented ceme- teries of medieval Christianity, and because Islam knows nothing of the communal tomb they are very extensive. Finally, there are the community pastures and the culti- vated fields.

This arrangement corresponds to a hierarchical social structure and is accompanied by a concentric arrange- ment of the different trades (see below) and different levels of the population distinguished by their position in society. At Lut, an Iranian oasis southeast of Kerman, Marco Polo described seven circles of concentric walls, protecting the various quarters, each of which was oc- cupied by the members of a single social class. Their social importance increased as they approached the citadel. From the outside to the center they were peasants of the oasis, foreigners (Tartars, Arabs, and Jews), armorers and smiths, caravaners, tradesmen and shopkeepers of the bazaar, warriors, and doctors of law.

Exceptions to this general scheme are unusual. One class of exceptions is the Mzabite villages of North Africa. These heretical Kharijites, who fled into the desert, built their towns with an eye to the necessity of defending them. They retained, to be sure, the egglike shape of the town, growing out from a center by the addition of successive circles in which the various elements of the population are arranged in hierarchical order; but the market, the economic center of the community, has been pushed to the very outskirts of town, indeed, out of the town itself.

This concentric arrangement presents certain disadvantages. The squeezing together of the various zones prevents the harmonious expansion of the city. The city's growth is hindered particularly by the stiff collar of cemeteries, which modern Islamic towns have had the greatest difficulty in breaking through, to the accompaniment of theological arguments beyond number. Some new districts have had to develop outside this empty belt and separated from the old commercial center. In these suburbs one finds wide commercial streets where different trades exist more or less in isolation, as contrasted with the complexity and ramification of the old bazaar, and where, naturally enough, one does not find the range and variety of occupations which surround the bazaar.

In fact, the second fundamental characteristic of the Islamic town is the ordering of the different trades into a hierarchy, with most of them physically separated from other trades and concentrated among their own kind. Right next to the great mosque are found the sellers of candles, incense, and perfumes, then the booksellers and bookbinders. In this general district are also the noblest trades. The *kaisariye* (the word comes from *Caesar*, meaning a former basilica, a double row of rooms and workshops opening on a central space) is a warehouse where clothing and materials are sold in big transactions. Then come the workmen in leather, the makers of slippers, then the tailors, the rug and tapestry salesmen, the jewelers. Still farther from the center are those who deal in foodstuffs—butchers, fruit and vegetable sellers—then the carpenters, locksmiths, and coppersmiths. Blacksmiths and potters are generally at the gates of the city, along with the sellers of wool thread and packsaddles, the saddlers and basket makers, whose clientele is mainly rural or nomadic.

This concentration of the different trades, though it is notable, is far from absolute. Certain very numerous trades are likely to escape localization, for example, tailors, slipper makers, weavers; and also certain very important trades, for example, bakers, grocers, porters, farriers, smiths, and potters (at Fez the smiths, who were once concentrated in a single district, have spread out with the growth of the town). Finally, there are certain trades the very nature of which requires dispersion, for instance, millers and tanners, who are found along the banks of streams. Even at the heart of the residential district, where economic life is at its simplest and most primitive, one encounters a tendency toward small commercial groupings, where in a single small area there may be a grocer, a fruit and vegetable dealer, a seller of charcoal, and a sweets merchant. Only the bakers of bread are really scattered about freely.

This grouping of the trades is accompanied by a division of territories. According to L. Massignon, this division is almost absolute in any given Islamic city throughout its history. But this view is too restrictive. At Cairo and at Damascus certain districts have been given over to the same occupations ever since the Middle Ages. But others have seen changes. At the time when Fostat was transferred to Cairo, the workmen in heavy materials stayed at Fostat, while the markets for slaves, cloth, and spices moved at once into the new capital.

Finally, a third characteristic of Islamic towns is segregation into districts of different ethnic and religious groups. Everywhere the residential districts are divided into closed units, consisting of lateral courtyards and alleys leading off a main street, which can be closed at either end by great gates. From the very beginning of the Islamic era this segregation appears among the different tribes of the conquering armies as a way of preventing race riots. It is still to be seen in North Africa at Tlemcen, where the Berber Hadri and the Turkish Kul-oghli occupy separate quarters; or at Mzab, where, around the districts of the Berber town, which is divided according to the original *soffs*, there have grown up the quarters of the Arab traders, first set up outside the gates and today incorporated within the circle of the city. But it is in the Near East, a mosaic of cultures and creeds, that segregation is pushed to the limit. J. Weulersse describes the forty-five different districts of Antioch, the aristocratic quarters of the

Turkish agas at the center, then Christian quarters, Greek
Orthodox and Armenian quarters, and Alawite quarters.
The city is a collection of cities living under the haunting
fear of general massacre. Segregation was also the rule in
the Balkans. There the desire for segregation was always
felt by the Turks, whereas the Christians had no particular fear of taking up residence in Moslem districts. So it
was in Sofia, where the steady advance of Bulgarians who
rented in Turkish quarters caused a retreat on the part of
the Turks, who as early as the seventeenth century were
abandoning their properties to avoid unbelieving neighbors. Certain mosques were the only traces left of an ancient Turkish population, and an edict of 1669 allowing
Bulgarians to move into Turkish quarters where the
population had radically diminished made the change
official. This Turkish reaction was typically that of a
colonizing minority; with time it grew less determined.
In 1878 there were streets in Sofia where Bulgarians,
Turks, Jews, Tartars, and others all lived together. But
in Anatolian towns segregation remained a vital force for
many years, and the Greek and Armenian quarters were
distinctive areas of towns throughout all Asia Minor until
the great population shifts took place after the First
World War and the Turko-Greek War which followed.
Everywhere the Moslem city appears to be crucially
lacking in essential unity; it is an assembly of disparate
elements set alongside one another without any real bonds
of unity.

The irregularity in detail of the city plan. Although
the Moslem town possesses a strong and distinct general
framework, the latter is generally obscured by an en-

tanglement of detail which seems quite inextricable. Especially in residential districts are the streets nearly always tortuous in the extreme. They bear very significant names, sometimes, like the Alley of the Twelve Windings in the once-Moslem town of Malaga. Onto these streets open a number of dead-end alleys, blind passages leading into inner courts, at the entrances to which a couple of dogs are always snarling and which represent a safe retreat for family life. The streets are just as narrow as they are twisting. Islam has never conceived of the street as a passageway for vehicles; at most it is for beasts of burden. At Istanbul in the middle of the nineteenth century not only carriages but even horses had trouble getting through certain streets. The Street of the Divan, widest in the city at that time, was no more than 9 or 10 feet wide in certain places. In many Moslem towns the roofs of houses on opposite sides of a street may touch at the eaves. Everywhere one finds covered passageways, little bridges over the streets. The frequent projections of the houses into the streets, their intrusive decorations and corbelings, make the circulation of traffic even more troublesome. Often two donkeys cannot get by one another. Two men may meet with the same difficulty. Furthermore, Moslem cities have very few empty spaces or open areas, a circumstance which does nothing to simplify the parking problem.

What then are the reasons for this state of affairs so clearly detrimental to a comfortable urban life? The specifically religious ideas of Islam, which do nothing to encourage urban display and which have played an important role (as we shall see later) in determining the type

of house that was built, have had some influence in the
matter of streets. A prescript of the Prophet requires a
minimum of 7 cubits (about 10 feet) as the width of
streets, a space that would permit the passing of two
heavily laden animals. This was the width chosen by
Caliph Omar for the regular streets of Basra and
Kufa and then in use at Baghdad, whereas the avenues
were up to 20 cubits (nearly 30 feet) wide, separating
blocks of houses up to 100 feet in depth. At Istanbul
during the first days of the conquest the Turks did
not modify the system of roads inherited from the Byzantines and continued, at least as late as the end of the
reign of Suleiman the Magnificent, to maintain broad
ways between their own new buildings. Such is the road
which still remains between the mosque of Shah-zadé
and the college of Ibrahim Pasha, or in the street known
as Mimar Sinan near the mosque Suleimaniye.

There even appeared in many cities of Islamic origin,
at least at the beginning, a remarkable care for organization, a strict order, a plan firmly laid out. This is the case
in many Moroccan cities. Salé, founded in 1610 by
Moorish refugees from Hornachos (Estremadura) and
from Andalusia, still exhibits today a regular plan (no
doubt due to the Spanish influence), with four main
roads running north-south and two crossroads running
east-west. But the same regularity of design also existed
on the other bank of the Bou Regreg, at Rabat, founded
alongside an ancient ribat in 1195 by the third Almohad
caliph, Yaqub al-Mansur. It was established "on the
model of Alexandria," with streets which ran straight
and parallel and intersected one another only at right

angles. And if this plan, which today is almost wholly effaced, was attributed at the time to Al-Mansur's taste for "the strange and the enormous," his example was far from being unique. At Meknès and at Taza, both Almohad in origin, one sees more or less clearly that the streets have been laid out according to the *qibla* (the orientation toward Mecca or to the east) of the mosque or to its perpendicular. The Almohad casbah of Marrakech and Fez Djedid (New Fez), a governing city created alongside ancient Fez, are other examples of planned cities. The plan generally adopted is something like a rectangle, no doubt because of the influence of the Hellenistic plan. This is true of all the Merinid towns that were built in Morocco during the fourteenth century, true in Tunisia, true of all the towns successively built on the site of Cairo from the camp of the Abbassid generals, which was founded in 748 north of Fostat and had east-west streets, to the Fatimid Cairo of the renegade Greek Djawhar (969–971), which had one great street, running south-southwest to north-northeast in the direction of the prevailing summer winds, and twenty side streets (seven were laid out by Djawhar himself), which reproduced the Hellenistic checkerboard. Likewise in the earlier town of Ibn Tulun arteries perpendicular and parallel to the main business street marked off that many properties, which were divided among the soldiers. But the circular-radial plan, which is certainly more in accord with the theocratic ideas of Islam, has sometimes been realized, as in the first Islamic centers at Kufa and at Basra, in the Abbassid Baghdad of Al-Mansur (762–763), and in certain Iranian towns. This circular plan, charged with ritual significance and according so well in Iran with the ancient traditions of the country (cf. the plan of Ecbatana, according to Herodotus) at the same time that it corresponded nicely with the Islamic ideal, nonetheless yielded to the rectangular plan in the Maghreb and Egypt, where the classical tradition remained in force.

These many examples will suffice to show that in most cases the irregular plans of Islamic towns represent an acquired rather than a congenital characteristic. Yet an excellent student of Spanish-Moslem towns (L. Torres-Balbas) has gone so far as to seek in the Yemen area of Arabia an origin for the city plan with blind alleys and twisting streets, which he thinks corresponds with a preconceived notion of the human spirit. As for conditions of insecurity, it is always possible that they played a role. The blind-alley arrangement makes for easy defense. It seems to have been complementary to segregation into districts. In desert cities like Es Sukhne, a little oasis in Syria, twisted streets appear as a defense against the Bedouins, who otherwise could paralyze the whole city by raking its streets with enfilading fire. The same thing may apply to certain little Iranian towns near the desert such as Birjand. But these are mainly local considerations. Even at Es Sukhne the origins of the agglomeration seem to have been linked to two parallel and regular streets which descended toward the watering point. The need for defense cannot be held generally responsible for the irregularity of the city plan.

Some people (e.g., E. Pauty) have likewise maintained that cities which sprang up spontaneously and grew naturally, without any preconceived order, were much more numerous in Islamic countries than towns created according to a regular plan imposed from above. But this is the idea of an architect concerned with describing the present appearance of cities, not that of a historian interested in the circumstances of their origin and growth. It is a fact that the original plan was often erased very quickly, though less quickly in the princely towns, which were relatively protected from individual initiative. Thus at Fez Djedid the original arrangement of the town can still be seen, though it has been partly filled in here and there with private dwellings. But the apparent predominance of spontaneous disorder over the original system certainly results less from an original deficiency than from a subsequent and separate evolution. It is a result of the absence of a municipal organization in Islamic countries. The city which springs up spontaneously and which, in countries with vigorous municipal organizations, evolves order out of disorder by means of successive reorganizations here never arrives at a clear self-discipline, while the town created by decree loses the basic pattern of its original foundation.

This is also the consequence of a certain legal attitude in Islam, well described by R. Brunschvig (in discussing Malikite law). Respect for public property on which no buildings stand is enjoined by a prescript of the Prophet; but the views of jurists are infinitely subtler. A purely formal condemnation of all encroachments on the public way is subject to important modifications; for example, one can acquire property simply by occupying it for a period of time (sixty years, according to the Malikite doctor of law Sahnun). Above all, the absence of an effective system of fines and damages encourages a general laxity as long as people can make their way through the public streets. The legal source of this laxity about usurpations on the public domain is an extension of a householder's property rights to cover the immediate vicinity of his house (*fina*); over this area he maintains preferential rights of occupation, permanent or temporary. So long as the public way can be used without appreciable hindrance, one can pre-empt bits of it freely. Most of the legal experts take the same line with regard to projections and overhangs. The whole process was seen very clearly by the French traveler Thévenot, who wrote in 1657: "There is not a single fine street in Cairo, but a number of little ones, which make many turns and detours; thus it is clear that all the houses were built without a general plan, each taking as much room as its builders needed, without considering whether it encroached on a public way or not." Only when the central power was weak did cities grow up irregularly from the very beginning. Examples are the two Turkish cities of the eighteenth century, Nevsehir ("New town") founded in 1720 and Yozgat founded in the second half of the century.

How then does the change from order to disorder come about? One must not simply hold the Moslem invaders responsible. At Aleppo and Damascus the degradation of the city plan had begun as early as the Byzantine era. Often it did not begin until some time after the Moslem conquest. At Istanbul it started only toward the end of the sixteenth century. Only after this era did streets tend to lose the fine width that they had under Suleiman the Magnificent and to become the wretched little alleys, sometimes less than six feet wide, which were common at the beginning of the nineteenth century. In fact one must presume an evolution in two stages, such as was well distinguished by G. Bartsch for Anatolian towns, and above all for Kayseri. First there was a stage of decadent urban life, linked to the conquest, in which the population diminished and buildings were abandoned; then there was a new burst of building, without order or rule, in which earlier alignments were not respected. At Istanbul the new masters installed themselves almost at random in an immense, almost empty city, through which they scattered freely their little wooden houses. Only later did the growth in population and the continued use of houses unsuitable to large cities lead to congestion and disorder. Then the regions around public monuments and mosques became choked, thanks to the weakness of those who administered pious foundations. Not only the empty spaces around the mosques but the courtyards within them were leased to commercial proprietors, and the bases of the minarets of Santa Sophia itself were rented to a confectioner, who kept his kettles there!

There were a few exceptions to this decadence. The princely towns, as we have remarked, had less trouble in retaining their original layouts. But for the most part the ancient pre-Islamic city plans disappeared entirely. This process was particularly swift in the commercial districts, the bazaars, where fragile, temporary shops multiplied quickly without regard for pre-existing boundaries. It was slower in the case of residential quarters, where builders had a special interest in following the outlines of ancient buildings in order to make use of their foundations (as in Aleppo). The ancient plans often survived with astonishing clarity in rural districts, where the Hellenistic quadrilaterals, maintained as divisions of olive groves and gardens in spite of the modern roads which cut through them, have served as a basis for recent construction (as in the area northeast of Antioch).

We must also note the remarkable anomaly provided by the pilgrimage towns of Arabia. Jidda and Mecca are towns without blind alleys; they are traversed by a network of streets which often intersect at right angles. Thus paradoxically, as E. F. Gautier has emphasized, they are towns of very little Islamic character. Without following this scholar in seeking the explanation in pre-Islamic cultural influences, in the psychology and habits of the Himyarites, whose interests centered on the Indian Ocean and the world beyond and who had little in common with the rest of the Islamic world, perhaps we can explain this unusual circumstance by simply pointing to the need for moving large crowds through these pilgrimage towns. Unlike the usual Moslem town, which is simply a scene for the unfolding of family life, they had to be built for the movement of great masses of people.

Apart from these exceptions, irregularity and anarchy seem to be the most striking qualities of Islamic cities. As J. Sauvaget has noted, the fundamental institutions of urban life have retained only the form given them by antiquity. Islam has been able to substitute for them nothing of its own. It simply copies. The *souks* come from the colonnaded avenue, the *kaisariye* and the *khan* from the basilica, the *hammam* from the thermae or ancient baths. Islam did not invent the bazaar, an ancient institution in the Near East, nor did it invent segregation into districts, which was a living principle in the medieval town and reached its apex in the cities founded by the Genoese on the Black Sea, on the very edge of the Islamic world. The effect of Islam is essentially negative. It substitutes for a solid and unified collectivity a shifting and inorganic assemblage of districts; it walls off and divides up the face of the city. By a truly remarkable paradox this religion that inculcates an ideal of city life leads directly to a negation of urban order.

Islam and the city house. Even in the realm of domestic urban architecture the influence of Islam has been prevailingly conservative and negative, limiting itself essentially to the retention of ancient influences and hostility toward more modern forms of urban dwelling.

Islam is fundamentally hostile, in the first place, to luxurious dwellings, and above all to lofty ones, which are symbols of pride and arrogance. From the days of Omar this rule has been strictly observed. In order to maintain world dominion, the Arab must reject luxury, must have only a provisional dwelling place, simple and humble. The low-built house is characteristic of Islam, in contrast with the lofty buildings characteristic of our cities since the Renaissance. At Istanbul regulations limited the height of Moslem houses to 10 cubits (about 16 feet) and those of non-Moslems to 8 cubits (a little more than 13 feet), and this rule was in effect as late as the *Tan-*

zimat (an organic statute initiating reforms in the Turkish Empire) in the middle of the nineteenth century. Big
buildings, such as apartment dwellings, are rare in Islamic countries. They are limited to certain of the central districts of the very largest towns, where they are
required by the density of the population. The *rab'*, or
"block," of Cairo gives lodging to a great many poor
families, but it is rarely found in other Arab cities. At
Fez it appears, by way of exception, in the central quarters of the *medina*, or "city," where space is crowded
and land prices high. On the other hand, it is characteristic of the Jewish quarters of North African towns, which
are strictly limited in extent and so obliged to build high.
Here one finds houses with several stories, tiny courtyards, and many windows; they are usually painted yel-
low or blue. The pilgrimage towns, Jidda and Mecca,
are well acquainted with multiple dwellings; there the
urban landscape is dominated by large buildings com-
parable to those in European towns and divided within
into many small apartments or independent rooms, each
with its kitchen. These houses have no central court but
open onto the street by means of vast bays in order to
take advantage of the fresh sea breezes. The owners
here have clearly built with an eye to the needs of hotel
keeping.[1]

Just as it proscribes the house of several stories, Islam
has also encouraged the use of fragile and perishable materials. E. F. Gautier has written many brilliant pages on

[1] "Skyscrapers" of eight or more floors are found in cities of
the Hadhramaut and buildings almost as high in Sana, the capital
of Yemen, but these are pre-Islamic in origin.

the architecture of Islamic countries. There houses are built for man—not for Allah. Despite the modesty commanded by piety, buildings must be built spectacularly —and quickly. Concern for durability is secondary. The use of fragile materials is a token of the insubstantiality of material things and the unimportance of the individual. In Mediterranean countries, on the other hand, the house of stone, made to stand forever, is linked to the life of the city and testifies to the builder's sense of having centuries ahead of him. Islamic architecture is an architecture of show, seductive but precarious and built for a single life. Hence the predominance of light materials, of clay, mud, or wood. At Istanbul little wooden houses scattered in gardens and many-colored wooden villas (*yalis*) on the banks of the Bosporus began to replace the solid brick constructions of the Byzantines immediately after the conquest. (The danger of fire did not appear until later when the wooden buildings became crowded on top of one another.) There are few exceptions to the rule that Islam builds with fragile materials. The *souks* of Aleppo were made of durable materials, but they were made for European traders.

As for the layout of houses, the prescription against height and the use of fragile materials have encouraged the persistence of a pre-Islamic plan, the house with a central court or patio, derived from the Greek house with a peristyle. This design has continued to dominate Arabian Egypt, the Maghreb (where it reproduces the African house of the first centuries of the Christian era), and Moslem Spain. This house is very different from the Roman house with an atrium, a room with its ceiling

pierced by a rectangular opening. For no particular
reason this style seems to dominate certain areas, such as
Marrakech. Islam has also transmitted various Near
Eastern influences, which are visible in the Tunisian
house, a rectangle with two lateral galleries along the
patio. But Algerian and Moroccan houses are typically
peristyle houses. This basic concept can still be felt beneath the profusion of *iwans*, or "cloisters," the reinforcements, and the corbelings which are no doubt Near
Eastern in origin but which have expanded with Islam
as far as the Maghreb. Turkish Islam, for its part, has
known scarcely anything but two-story houses, derived
directly from country houses and characterized, in these
relatively cold climates, by a double installation, with
winter quarters on the ground floor and summer quarters
upstairs. Houses with central courts are exceptional in
Turkey; they represent the caprices of governors in
Arab provinces who returned to Anatolia or of merchants who became familiar with this type of house in
the course of their travels.

As for the organization of family life, the general
adoption of an L-shaped entry marks the jealous defense
by Islam of the family's privacy. (In Turkish Croatia
another solution to this problem prevails; Moslem houses
there are distinguished by a great wooden fence that
shuts off the court.) But the fundamental problem was
how to divide the interior into two sections, the *haremlik*
(for women) and the *selamlik* (for men and masculine
visitors). The Hellenistic ground plan with its peristyle,
the house with a patio, was ill-adapted to this division,
for it was hard there to find a special place to reserve

for the women. Several solutions were adopted. In the Turkish two-story house the *haremlik* is often on the ground floor protected by a hall, whereas the *selamlik* is on the upper story at the head of the stairway. In particularly well-to-do households there are sometimes two separate buildings joined by a covered corridor (*mabeyn*). In simple houses of a single story *haremlik* and *selamlik* are generally separated by a central hall corridor, off either side of which the living quarters open. In Arab countries a house with two courts has sometimes been developed, one court for men, the other for women; and in Cairo one finds houses with two *qaʿah* (rooms covered with skylights and little cupolas, lighted from above and entered from the court). In the same city two-story houses, unlike those in Turkey, have the *haremlik* on the upper floor. In Baghdad one finds the house with two courts, the larger one being the women's or the men's, depending on whether the proprietor's family or public life is more important. In middle-class houses with a single court the *haremlik* is generally raised a few steps above the rest of the house. But usually no special arrangement has been adopted, and Islam has thus taken over a type of city house not particularly adapted to its needs.

Islam's influence in spreading the popularity of this house has, however, been eminently positive. The taste of Islam for city living has spread specifically urban dwellings into even the little towns and villages, which in Moslem countries quickly take on a citified look, the appearance of being cities in miniature. Nowhere, perhaps, is this clearer than in the interior of Africa, where

the look of rural communities changes completely the
moment one passes from Islamic regions to those of
animism. On the upper Ivory Coast the villages of the
Mandes (Moslems isolated in a fetishist area) continue
to present far toward the south a remarkably urban appearance, with their grilled windows and their narrow
and twisting streets between gray houses with roof terraces. Although cubic buildings of clay, of an urban appearance, were doubtless pre-Islamic in origin, Islam certainly contributed greatly to their spread.

The Evolution of Islamic Cities

It is obvious that the structure of these traditional Islamic cities is not at all compatible with the demands of
modern life, above all with traffic on a level beyond that
of human porters and beasts of burden. But whereas our
European towns, conquered in good time by the vehicle
and continually supervised and closely corrected by
public power, generally adapted themselves without too
much trouble, the maze of the Islamic city called for
something like a surgical operation. It was necessary to
cut the old cities to the very bone or, failing that, to
build new ones beside them. These two solutions (internal reorganization of the old cities by a slow or sudden process and the building of new towns of a European
character beside the ancient centers) have been combined in different proportions, but the second is not
distinctively Islamic. The new cities have often been
built by colonizers from Europe itself. Even when they
were built by local people, or when the Islamic upper
crust came to inhabit them, at least in part, after they

were built, the life led there and the organization of the city have nothing about them specifically Islamic. It is the first type of evolution that most particularly invites our attention.

First signs of change and beginnings of urbanization. Without direct influence arising from prolonged contact with the Occident, Moslem cities have almost never changed of their own accord. Exceptional problems of traffic and transport have been met by casual or improvised measures. So it was at Cairo, according to the author of the *Tarikh Djafari*, where the Fatimid Caliph Al-Hakim had a great chandelier made which he desired to send to the mosque of Amr. Men had to be sent out in advance, we are told, to destroy all obstacles filling the streets, to tear down façades and balconies, and to widen the roads which the transport was to take. In 1813 the same thing had to be done for the parade that followed the marriage of the pasha's daughter. In the Moorish villages of Spain rather less radical measures were followed. As horsemen could not pass through the streets of Granada with lance in hand, the Moors had holes cut in their houses, especially at street corners, to let lances through; and rules had to be promulgated forbidding the construction of arcades which impeded the movements of men on horseback. But all this was merely trivial cosmetic work on the face of chaos.

Turkey manifested the first impulses toward urbanization, the achievement of the "enlightened" sultans of the end of the eighteenth and the beginning of the nineteenth centuries. Selim III, in connection with his efforts at a military revival, built a special district beside the

barracks that bear his name, with geometrically regular
streets and mod l houses on every street corner. In 1837
Von Moltke, the Prussian military adviser of Mahmud II,
drew up the first plan for Istanbul at the instance of the
sultan, but his recommendations for replacing wooden
houses with ones of stone or brick, for widening streets
and squares, and for clearing the mosques and building
new wharves remained a dead letter. In 1847–1848 the
Turks were still not leaving more than 12 to 20 feet for
public streets, whereas Von Moltke's project had called
for a minimum width of 27 feet. And the fact that men
could now build as high as they wished, because the old
Islamic rules against high buildings were withdrawn in
1839, rendered the need for wider streets more obvious.

It was, in fact, the influence of the western world
which brought about the first movements to transform
the Islamic city. The dates of this impulse are extremely
variable. Whereas the Christian reoccupation set off a
transformation of Spanish towns, an equivalent change
in North Africa had to wait until the beginnings of
French colonization. For military reasons the French
governors of Cairo dismantled the gates separating different districts about 1801, but the beginnings of major
modifications go back to Mehemet Ali (viceroy, 1805–
1848). In Turkey the decisive impulse was linked to the
Crimean War and to the problems posed by the passage
of allied troops through Istanbul; thus the first efforts
at urbanization took place in the Ottoman provinces during the 1860's. Although Russian colonization had a profound effect on the cities of Turkestan, those of Iran had
to await the reign of Riza Shah Pahlevi (r. 1925–1941)

before any serious efforts at modernization were made.

Principal phases of evolution. When ancient urban settlements are to be modernized, it is customary for the work to be done in distinct stages. The first stage is always to demolish the architectural incrustations, the balconies, galleries, and projections of every sort so frequent in Moslem architecture. In the Moorish towns of Spain, Catholic kings from the sixteenth century on made furious war on corbelings in the name of the new aesthetic of the Renaissance, with its desire for order, regularity, symmetry. King John forbade projecting cornices at Toledo. At Malaga the galleries of the tradesmen's quarters were destroyed in 1501. Orders to realign the streets followed, and the ostentation of façades soon replaced the austerity of the blind walls which had marked previous dwellings. So also at Cairo, where Mehemet Ali set about the work of reform by abolishing *mastabas,* those stone benches which, when placed in front of shops, effectively diminish the width of the streets.

The second stage is that of great thoroughfares. It begins with the growth of interurban traffic and the pressing necessity of making passage through towns easier. New Street in Cairo was opened in 1845 to provide a main thoroughfare into the old city; it was barely wide enough for two loaded camels to pass, and a wheeled vehicle was rarely seen on it. About the middle of the last century thoroughfares began to be numerous. An Ottoman governor, Midhat Pasha, made his presence felt in many places. He is responsible for the great arteries of Islamic Sofia, which were built about 1860; they are not only a means of crossing the city but extensions of the

great routes across the Balkans. From the city's outer
gates they lead to its very center, where they all come
together in the heart of the bazaar. Between 1860 and
1870 Midhat Pasha, with the aid of his subordinate, Esad
Pasha, put through a number of realignments of houses,
the owners of which often lost at least half of their property without the slightest recompense. They were only
too happy to escape the vast fires that were burning up
the Turkish towns at this time and that, so it was said,
the central authorities sometimes allowed to spread freely
in order to clear some open space. Midhat Pasha was also
responsible a little later for the first main thoroughfares
in Damascus. In Iran, Riza Pahlevi's first efforts at urbanization took very much the same form. Except for the
timid attempts at modernization by Nasr-ed-Din Shah in
Teheran in the last third of the nineteenth century, there
was not a single street in any Iranian town which ran
more than sixty feet in a straight line until Riza Pahlevi
assumed the throne, and then suddenly great square grill-
works of streets were imposed on cities as on the tops of
gigantic cakes, with a minimum of consideration for even
the largest complexes of public buildings. This modernization was incomplete because it was limited to the main
roads. As it was often accompanied by a lowering of the
roadbed, the little streets now appeared to be suspended
high above the main streets. Bridges were often attached
to the main arteries as a way of extending them. At Istanbul the first concern of the municipal commission created
in 1855 was to enlarge the Karakoy Bridge between
Istanbul and Galata; this was done in 1857. The next
order of business was to disencumber Karakoy Square,

where up to that time it had been barely possible for two loaded animals to pass one another.

The third stage is the opening up of the commercial districts and the freeing of the public buildings, a process which generally takes place before any serious alterations are made in the residential quarters. In the cities of Turkestan the Russians carved out great thoroughfares into the bazaars, such as the new avenue which, coming from the European town, heads straight for the heart of Samarkand, Registan Square, passes around one of its corners, burrows through the bazaar from end to end, and finally goes to the other end of the city. The public monuments at the center of towns are thus improved, while the traditional appearance of the residential districts is hardly changed at all. At Istanbul the freeing of public buildings came gradually after an 1864 regulation went into effect forbidding the administrators of pious foundations to lease any property or do any new building in the immediate neighborhood of the mosques. Bit by bit the vicinities of Santa Sophia and of the mosque of Sultan Ahmet were cleared; the mosque of Fatih was disencumbered by means of a fire. Since 1938 work has been in progress, at great expense, to clear the New Mosque (Yeni Jami) in the quarters near the Karakoy Bridge.

In the last stage of modernization, along with a very slow modification of the old residential districts, some changes occur in the style of the houses. Often the first efforts to regularize a city do not really involve a Europeanizing of it. The new buildings are all of a traditional type. At Meshed in northeastern Iran, the new buildings are marked by an extraordinary indulgence of fantasy in the Iranian style. The capital, Teheran, is more severe. The first postrevolutionary Ankara (Ankara of 1923–1930) is also a museum of buildings in pseudo-Moorish style, covered with flowery decorations and complicated ornaments. In the great buildings of modern Islam there still persist various corbelings and stone balconies that reproduce those of the old wooden houses. The western style of apartment houses is a late adoption. In Meshed the first houses in the western style on the main streets followed a colonial Russian pattern; they were broad houses of a single story, with square windows. The change was more abrupt at Jidda, where the local style was favorable to a change-over, and big modern apartment houses replaced the old, several-storied pilgrims' houses without any perceptible adjustment having to be made. But after these old Islamic towns have been transformed, they often leave one with the impression of something fragmentary, something unfinished. Houses of completely different styles are jumbled together. Between buildings several stories high nestle little shops. The town looks like one in process of renovation —a fact which gives to Islamic towns, paradoxically enough, the appearance of American cities.

Regional varieties of change. Different kinds of Moslem towns may be distinguished, according either to the stage of evolution which they have reached and the speed of that evolution or to the way in which they have mixed old forms with new ones.

a) The Spanish type. The Spanish Moslem towns changed masters in an era when the pressure of modern conditions was scarcely being felt. Despite the retouching noted above, much of it carried out for aesthetic reasons, the city plan was scarcely modified. The Islamic layout of streets, with its many dead ends, predominates in the plans made at the end of the eighteenth century (Seville 1771, Malaga 1791, Granada 1796, Cordova 1811). Even today traces of the old plan survive in the less-renovated quarters, as around the Alcazar in Seville or the great mosque in Cordova. And at Toledo the hilly contours of the city has forced streets to follow the same paths for many centuries. On the whole Spanish towns are distinguished by the remarkable slowness of their evolution, its progressive and gradual character, at least until the great redrawing of municipal plans which generally took place during the nineteenth century in the southern cities of the peninsula.

b) Radical transformations. Radically transformed towns are found in Algeria on the one hand and in the Balkans and in the northern (Pontic) part of Anatolia on the other hand, but there are extreme variations among them.

In Algeria the European occupation was originally precarious, and this is the reason why the newcomers settled into already existing towns instead of creating new ones. The consequence of this occupation, originally temporary, was the profound modification of one part of the cities, a change which grew steadily more sweeping as the occupation continued. At Algiers the whole lower town thus assumed, through the cutting out of streets and the construction of European-style apartment houses, the aspect of a new town with a regular plan.

Actually very little is left of the Algerian towns that existed before the coming of the colonizers: only the upper part of Algiers (the casbah), the southern districts of Constantine, and a few isolated areas of old Tlemcen. Everywhere else the renovation has been complete.

The Balkan solution was generally the same, since Christian reoccupation took place at the time of a new era in traffic management. The most extreme example is that of Sofia, where the Ottoman city of 1878, which had nearly 30,000 inhabitants, was practically wiped out. But, strangely enough, the same type of solution prevailed in cities that remained Moslem, the Turkish towns of northern Anatolia and the Pontic districts—everywhere where the use of wooden houses, liable to repeated destructive fires, made a city susceptible to widespread devastation.

The evolution of Istanbul constitutes a particularly remarkable example. Here we have statistics from the beginning of the municipal commissions. From 1858 to 1865, 160 fires destroyed no fewer than 4,114 houses. The great fire of September 4, 1865, which ravaged the greater part of the city, from Sirkedji to Kum Kapu, was followed shortly by two others. In all, 3,551 houses were burnt that year, and four-fifths of the city was reduced to the state of open fields and waste regions, from the Golden Horn to Marmara, from Santa Sophia to the mosque of Bajazet. This was the occasion for the first significant widening of streets that the city had ever known. A quarter of the burnt-over area was taken, without reimbursement, for the laying out of streets, which were immediately widened from about 12 to more than 40 feet. Other fires, which continued till the end of the First World War, were the source of many improvements. The Christian suburb of Pera was not spared, and its great fire destroyed 3,000 houses. A climax was reached in the decade from 1908 to 1917 when seventy-nine great fires on the two banks of the Golden Horn destroyed at least 25,000 houses. Of these, 7,500 were in the quarter of Fatih and 2,400 in the district of Aksaray in the Turkish city. Recently established wide avenues lined with apartment houses have converted these ancient burnt-out areas into the most modern districts of the city. The rebuilding is far from complete, not only because there is little pressure from a growing population, but also because the new housing makes possible an enormous increase in the number of people who can be accommodated on a single piece of land. Thus the rebuilt areas are right next to pieces of waste land and the old scattering of little wooden houses in the unburnt districts, giving the city a look entirely its own.

This type of change took place throughout the Balkans (the appearance of Salonika was completely changed by the great fire of 1917) and in all the towns throughout Marmara and along the Black Sea, where fires, like those of Balikesir and Gerze recently destroyed several thousand buildings. In the rest of Anatolia, where houses are made of stone and hardened clay, changes have been much less radical. The notable and always sensible effort of modern Turkey to urbanize itself is marked everywhere by an attempt to place wide avenues next to old quarters, or around them, and to line these avenues with modern villas and parks. The region of the railroad station and the main highways are often treated in the same way.

c) Moderate changes and juxtapositions. The next type of change is marked by a much greater respect for the ancient urban centers. It is found in Tunisia and Morocco and throughout the Near East, whether Arabian or Iranian. In Tunisia and Morocco the first work of colonialism was to build new cities independent of the old *medinas*. In Morocco, which was occupied later, the segregation was more complete and the towns were more sharply divided. In Tunisia, where European quarters had existed before the protectorate, new districts were built in the immediate proximity of the *medinas* and sometimes surrounding them. But in both cases change was continuous. In Morocco the empty spaces between *medinas* and modern quarters have by now generally been filled in. Everywhere new native suburbs, often shantytowns, encircle the modern quarters. The native towns themselves have not been changed a great deal. Thus at Fez an automobile can travel, not without difficulties, in the ghetto and more easily in Fez Djedid; but except for a very few peripheral areas the native city itself is almost entirely closed to it.

This system of juxtaposing old and new characterizes almost all the great cities of the Arabian Near East. When a colonizing power has not clearly asserted its will, the development of new districts has generally taken place in a somewhat disorderly way. In Cairo the new districts with their geometric plans have been added since the time of Mehemet Ali. They are west of the old city, toward the Nile, and northwest. On the outskirts satellite cities like Heliopolis show signs of division into lots. But here and there in the suburbs ancient and irregular fragments of city have been absorbed without being perceptibly transformed (for example, the greater part of Bulaq). At Damascus a new city, Salhiye, with wide geometrical streets, has set itself up next to the older town. Recent additions look like a suburb of a great modern city, even though districts dating from the Ottoman era maintain a strictly oriental appearance. Certain new cities of the Near East owe practically everything to European influence, for example, Alexandria, the plan of which is artificial in its entirety.

Transformations of ancient cities have been relatively clearer in Russian Turkestan, where an intermediate type of change, between the radical-transformation and juxtaposition types may be distinguished. New cities, products of Russian colonization, have certainly been created outside the pre-existing native towns, but at the same time the towns themselves have been profoundly altered, especially in the bazaars and central quarters, where the great monumental buildings are sometimes the only things to have been preserved.

Changes of structure. Have these changes in the appearance of Islamic towns been accompanied by any alterations in the structure of the population and in the relations of social classes within the city? So far as the population is concerned, it is worthy of note that the well-to-do classes are everywhere quick to abandon the ancient *medinas* for newly built districts. Morocco is an exception. There this change has scarcely begun, and the rich and conservative bourgeoisie have generally remained, as at Fez, in the ancient *medinas*. Everywhere else one finds that the upper classes have been quick to move out of the old districts and into the new ones built in the European style. In Istanbul this abandonment of the old wooden dwellings was accompanied by a steady invasion of Moslems into the Christian district of Pera. Generally the old districts become a proletarian quarter, less wholesome even than the shantytowns that grow up around the cities; this has been the common experience in Casablanca. The density of the population increases steadily in these slum districts, at least in proportion to the amount of living space available—as, for example, in the casbah of Algiers. Because the buildings are all low, many fewer people may inhabit a single acre of ground than in modern districts. In Algeria where the two populations live at particularly close quarters, the natives have invaded the oldest Christian quarters (the lower city of Algiers). But the contrary process (movement of Christian elements into the Moslem areas of the towns) has almost never taken place, and on this point segregation remains absolute. Even in a secular and Europeanized country like Turkey no non-Moslem elements live in the Moslem district of Istanbul to the south of the Golden Horn, if one excepts the ancient Greek quarter of Phanar, which has not changed since the taking of Byzantium.

With reference to commercial relations, the rise of new city complexes has not been without its influence on the traditional trade structure—not that the bazaars have been much changed. Standing at the central crossroads of the towns, they are stable in relation to their residential quarters so long as the quarters remain unchanged. The creation of new districts outside the city and of new suburbs has no other effect than to create new groups of autonomous trade centers without any transfer from the original center group. In the actual development relations have not been quite so rigid as this. The physical arrangement of the various trades has sometimes been upset by the introduction of imported objects, which change the layouts of the shops and the displays of merchandise, as well as by the demand for European goods in modern districts. The influence of the tourist traffic often produces a kind of dispersion of the different trades; the chief of the Fez bookbinders used to complain, even before the First World War, that one of his fellow craftsmen had moved out of the *souk* in order to have first crack at the tourists. As for the new districts, there is no concentration of craft centers in them. Shops there are likely to be interspersed with residences, and the business districts differ hardly at all from their European equivalents. At Casablanca, a new town, the men of a particular trade do not cluster together at all, unless perhaps it is the cloth merchants, a particularly noble and therefore "competitive" line. At Pera may be seen a curious grouping of electricians and sellers of automobile accessories along the one-way streets through which automobiles are practically obliged to pass. The result of having no fixed prices, and thus of bargaining over every object, is that the trades tend to stick together by way of guaranteeing "competition" for each buyer.

ISLAM AND THE EXPLOITATION
OF THE SOIL

Islam's negative attitude toward agriculture. As has already been said, Islam is a city dweller's religion. Mohammed belonged to the commercial, urban aristocracy of Mecca. Working the soil about oases was by definition a servile occupation. After the conquest in the lands newly annexed to Islam the countryside remained for a long time under the control of unbelievers, whereas the cities were centers of the faith. These circumstances may be seen in all the teachings of the Prophet. In the Koran the growth of crops is never viewed as the consequence of human labor but as the simple expression of divine will (for example, XXVI, 33–36, or LVI, 64–65—God is the true sower of seeds). The so-called "Oral Traditions" of Islam are filled with a spirit hostile to the peasantry. Seeing a plowshare, the Prophet is said to have remarked, "That never enters into the house of a believer without degrading it." If trees in general and palm trees in particular were never to be destroyed wantonly, it was nonetheless perfectly legitimate to cut them for general purposes or for use in warfare.[2] To be sure, there are texts on the other side of the question. "Every time that a Moslem plants a tree or sows a seed, he will be entitled to recompense should a bird, a man, or a beast eat anything from what grows," says one rescript.[3] "A man who has loved the soil passionately will receive permission in Paradise to cultivate and harvest crops more magnificent than mountains."[4] Other "traditions" show

[2] Bukhari, *The Book of Sowing*, 6.   [3] *Ibid.*, 1.
[4] *Ibid.*, 20.

the companions of the Prophet engaged in agricultural pursuits. But commerce and trade are always recommended more insistently. The merchant who is honest and worthy of faith is with the Prophet and the martyrs.

Islamic landholding practices and their consequences. Contradictory attitudes may be noted in Islamic legislation on the use of land. In its favor is the fact that the value of Moslem laws concerning land reclamation is indisputable. To gain possession of land it is not enough to occupy it; one must make it produce something. And, on the other hand, by putting abandoned lands under cultivation, one can gain possession of them. This doctrine is not altogether a disinterested one. After the conquests of Byzantium and the expansion beyond Arabia, a tax on crops became the basic financial resource of the state, which thus had a special interest in expanding the production of grain and diminishing the amount of land standing waste. This policy seems like an antidote to the system of landholding which grew out of imperial concessions (as we shall see later on), and which was eminently liable to change through shifts of princely favor, often leading to the abandonment of lands. The reclamation of deserted land, a prime means of acquiring new land under Islamic law, is thus a precious encouragement to agriculture.

We note, however, that the various schools of Moslem law take very different attitudes toward the details of this process. Shafiites and Malikites refuse to allow non-Moslems any claim to the rights of reclamation, though Hanafites and Hanbalites grant them. According to Abu Hanifa, the authority of the government is needed for reclamation, but Malik thinks it is necessary only in the vicinity of settlements; others consider it altogether unnecessary. It is true that certain disciples of Abu Hanifa (such as Abu Yusuf Yakub), more charitable than their master, consider that the permission of the government was given once for all and is henceforth universally valid. In the matter of taxation Abu Hanifa declares that the tithe (paid by Moslems) and the tribute (paid by non-Moslems) cannot be levied simultaneously on the same piece of ground. This is a precious bit of encouragement for non-Moslem farmers, as the other three doctors agree that both payments can be imposed simultaneously. Subtleties of this character are not without effect on the intensity with which the soil is cultivated; farming is much easier for non-Moslems where Hanafite legislation prevails than anywhere else. (This was certainly true of the immense Ottoman Empire.)

The darker side of Islamic legislation concerning agriculture brings us directly to the problem of the sharecropper, and more generally to the problems of leases and tenants. A certain number of prescripts formally condemn all leasing of land: "Let the man who possesses a piece of ground either work it himself or grant the use of it freely to others. If he does not do so, let him leave his land uncultivated" (a "tradition" ascribed to Rafi and Jabir). These texts have given rise to labyrinthine discussions among the doctors and have necessitated the most elaborate quibbles on the part of those who, for practical reasons, were convinced that a society of any maturity must necessarily have a system of landleasing and who sought to promote one. Bukhari in his com-

mentaries on this prescript tries to show that it describes
an action, clearly meritorious in itself, but not obliga-
tory, a gesture of generosity such as might be recommended to an elite body but not to the ordinary masses
of the faithful. Explicit as they are, these texts are also
opposed on the basis of other prescripts which show examples of sharecropping and tenantry among the close
associates of the Prophet. There is even a famous "tradition" with regard to the oasis of Khaybar which at-
tributes such practices to the Prophet himself, at least
in respect to date trees. Various doctors (among them
Bukhari) limit themselves to disapproving of contracts
considered too hazardous for the tenant, such as tenancy
in exchange for a stated quantity of fruit, or tenancy
with the landlord entitled to a specified fraction of the
land's produce. Others object to the leasing of unim-
proved land (*mouzaraa*) but allow the leasing of land
that has been planted (*mousakat*), while still others take
an exactly contrary position. Even "the contract of
planting" (*mougharasa*) is inadmissible.

Certainly this tangle of subtleties and limitations poses
a serious obstacle to the harmonious development of relations in the agrarian community. While the strict rule
against leases has been quietly forgotten or verbally cir-
cumvented, the rule against farming at a fixed rent, a
procedure infinitely more progressive and beneficial to
the peasantry, has never been relaxed, and this practice
has never taken root in any Islamic country. The exceptions to this rule are few and slight: in Iran, for example,
in the neighborhood of Yezd and Isfahan and in certain
regions of the Caspian provinces. In any case, this system

never develops except in lands that have been under cultivation for a very long time and where the average yield is almost exactly known; it is never found in lands newly opened up to agriculture. Paradoxically, this rule against fixed rents accounts in part for the spread throughout Moslem countries of leases based on a percentage of the yield (notably one-fifth), which are now found almost everywhere. It is true that by forbidding loans at interest Islam has removed from the lands under Moslem sway the blight that usury casts over Far Eastern landscapes; but the system of land tenure has nonetheless had a profound effect on social relations.

Finally, the conditions under which one holds property in land under Islamic law have contributed importantly to the general feeling against the land. The fundamental principle is that land belongs mainly to the state (the *miri* lands of the Ottomans) and cannot be alienated as far as it is a religious trust (the institution of *wakf*, or *habous* of North Africa). The origins of this system do not date back to the days of Mohammed, who at the beginning of the conquests divided new land among his warriors, but to Omar, who revived the old principle of collective tribal property in the form of "nationalization" of land by the central power. The term *wakf* originally had this meaning of the state's claim to own land, before it came to imply mortmain or a religious trust. The attitude of the different schools of law have varied with regard to these two ways of dividing the soil, both of which lay claim to equally venerable authority. For the Malikites, conquered territories are set up in *wakf* by the full authority of the law almost automatically. The Shafiites think that such lands should be divided among the conquerors according to the Prophet's own example, at least unless all those who would otherwise be beneficiaries are agreed upon putting their land into *wakf*. For the Hanafites, a choice between the two systems must be made by the government. In fact land administration as established by the Ottoman Empire was vested almost completely in the state, all the land being originally decreed *miri*. Here too, as in the land program of Omar, pre-Islamic tendencies reinforced the conceptions of Islam. A period of decadence, characterized in the feudal Anatolian states by the predominance of little domains and hereditary *wakfs*, gave rise to the Ottoman regime; the real derivation was direct from the earlier reign of the Seljuks, and its culture patterns conformed to those of tribal statism, as practiced by the Turks of Central Asia (see the work of O. Turan). The power of this system of land tenure appears to be linked to the fact that Islam here endorsed previously existing conceptions. And Islam was ready to do so, because its diffusion by nomad peoples made easy an acceptance of the principle that land is impersonal.

The consequences of this notion were important. State ownership of land leads directly to organization into *ikta's*, concessions of land granted to soldiers and officials on condition that they form a kind of rural militia. The original feature of the *ikta'* is that the emperor's relation to his tenant is almost entirely distinct from the land itself; the land involves neither services nor duties but simply a rent payment, which is determined by the central power. The possessor of the land, a timariot or spahi, thus has no real interest in improving the use of the land. Grandiose plans concerning land utilization and disposition are made far from the soil by the state, which in the Ottoman Empire freely moved entire populations and arranged the cultivation of the soil to suit its own strategic and military ends. The man who worked the land directly had little control over it. This Oriental regime totally ignored the bonds of personal interest that constituted the best part of western feudalism. Islam knows nothing of the lord's interest in his vassals or of any notion that vassals may be a reservoir of craft abilities rather than simply a source of income. Moreover, the rule of succession, even when these successions have become practically hereditary, ignores seniority, that other guarantee against the state's absolute power. The Islamic law of inheritance in its purity works against the concentration of fortunes in a few hands and the development of great estates, but in conjunction with an absolute rule far removed from the soil itself it culminates not only in the parceling out of great estates but in urban absentee landlordism. Thus the state's rule over land, at least as it was developed by the Osmanli Turks, proves in the end disastrous for all organization of rural life. It stifles that whole ferment of progress and change which takes place only among those who work the soil directly and which is one of the taproots of all capitalist initiative. This is certainly one of the deeper reasons for Islam's economic decadence. Since the *ikta‘* system began to decay, changes in the direction of great properties owned outright, those of the *tchiftlik* ("estate") type, have brought progress in many directions, but the weight of past centuries still hangs heavily over the countryside in the East.

The Ottoman conquests brought Islam into a number of Balkan countries, where its agrarian policy seems pretty much the direct expression of the conquest. The Romanian princes, tax collectors for the Sublime Porte, greatly augmented their pressure on the peasants under this new impulsion. Bondage to the soil appeared to be linked here to a fiscal and administrative system. Yet not everything about this system was black. Although it offered less incentive, the absence of feudal duties and the fixity of the rent often made it seem fairly tolerable to peasants who compared it with non-Islamic systems. In certain eras in the Balkans it even brought about migrations of serfs toward the Ottoman Empire, more especially since ancient agrarian institutions were generally respected by an Osmanli public law that was not at all formalist and very little influenced by purely religious considerations. But this policy in regard to land ended, just as did the inalienable *wakfs,* by suppressing all progress.

The legal tangle left by this system seems all but inextricable. "Throughout Turkey nobody knows what it is to own a piece of land. . . . The village populations live in the middle of fields which they cultivate without really knowing who is the owner of the land by which they live." So wrote Michaud in the middle of the nineteenth century in his letters from the East. The way out is not yet clear. Despite all the time that has elapsed since the reforms of *Tanzimat* were decreed, Turkey has not yet been able to finish drawing up a register of land deeds. The categories of lands are innumerable, the legal quarrels many. Lawyers do, literally, a land-office business. The land problem has provided an altogether unexpected source of trouble for French colonization in North Africa. From one point of view the fact that large areas of land seemed to be in the public domain should have made it easy to get them into production after an original act of colonial intervention; a case in point was the olive groves of Sfax. If the great areas of open land which might have been assigned either to the nomads or to the state had been clearly given to the state, this would have opened an immense field for colonizing activity. But more conservative policies won the day, and the *habous*, or collective ownership of most land, has clearly retarded the process of getting the lower steppe of Tunisia into production (cf. J. Despois).

Such then are the general ways in which Islam interferes with the organization of rural life. On a more limited scale, in the details of country living, its influence is no less inhibitory.

Forbidden foods and their consequences: (a) *Alcoholic drinks.* Islam's ban on alcoholic drinks as a whole and on wine in particular (only the Hanafites tolerate alcohol in any form; they limit the ban to wine) has had noteworthy effects on the agricultural countryside of the Mediterranean areas conquered by the Moslems. It has pushed toward the northwestern part of the Mediterranean the winegrowing industries that had previously been localized in the eastern part. As late as the high Middle Ages, the Syrian wines of Gaza and Zarephath exported by native merchants were much sought after in Merovingian Gaul. The ban on alcohol did not originally extend to the cultivation of vines, and the falling off in grape production was gradual. Yet it was very notable. Only in Moslem Spain, it would seem, did the growing of vines remain important. In Persia too the growing of grapes lingered long, and wine was sung by the Persian poet Hafiz. The Shiite heresy encouraged the continued drinking of wine in Persia, but in Azerbaijan, Shiraz and Isfahan, Khurasan and Teheran, the making of wines has always been almost entirely in the hands of Jews and Armenians. In 1889 a monopoly on the trade was conceded by the shah to Europeans, and it soon passed into the hands of some Belgians organized under the veiled name of "The General Society of Commerce and Industry in Persia." In Sicily, despite the Arab poetry in praise of wine which has come down to us, the decay of the trade was rapid, and before long the island had to import its wine from Naples. In Asia Minor wine production was almost entirely limited to Christian, Greek, and Armenian villages. In Crete the wine trade was completely destroyed by the Turkish conquest and by the partial Islamization of the populace. The Moslem invasion of the second half of the sixteenth century is popularly supposed to have ruined grape growing in Ethiopia. In Syria and North Africa the grapevine became a decorative garden plant. Among the Berber populations of the Kabyles and in the Rif it remained an important element of life, an integral part of the orchard, and was associated with the other fruit-bearing plants. Local stock was used mostly. But the drinking of wine almost disappeared. It barely survived as a practice among the Riffians, the Beni Iguinssen, and the Beni Mezguelda. Elsewhere in Islam the custom is also found among certain other mountain-dwelling peoples, among the Shiite Ahl-i-Hakks of Kurdistan, among the Yazidis, and among Ismaili of the Upper Indus like the Hunza, all heretical sects.

Even among Christian peoples the growing of wine grapes was ruined by the imposition of excessive taxes. The most remarkable example is that of Cyprus, where at the time the British took over the winegrowers were staggering under a veritable torrent of special taxes. There were a tax on the grape harvest, a tax on the amount of wine produced, a surtax on transportation, and a tax of 10 per cent ad valorem after the product of the whole district had been assessed. In addition, the long waiting periods at the government office at Limassol where the wine was to be weighed ultimately gave it the taste of goatskin, which rendered it all but unfit for exportation. Under these circumstances it was barely possible to make a profit. For reasons like these men abandoned the growing of grapes on the high rugged meadows on the southern slope of Troodos, where the vine was practically the only thing that could be grown at all. In fact all regions under the political control of Islam saw their wine-making industries disappear, and the vine became a plant grown only in the mountains, more or less integrated with the Mediterranean flora and the local way of life, but never capable of supplying even a reasonable export demand. From the plains the vine retreated to the mountains, from the open fields to the gardens.

Farther east Syria during the seventeenth and eighteenth centuries became an importer of quality wines for the use of European colonists, thus reversing the trade picture of the early Middle Ages, even though grapes were still planted in the mountains. During the same period the Franks of Constantinople got their supplies of wine from Tenedos and Santorin (now Thera), and the little Greek islands held a monopoly on the export of wine from the Levant, since they were freer of the labyrinthine legislation of the Ottoman Empire than other areas were. From this period dates the reputation of wine from Samos, the island where in olden times Strabo found everything excellent *except* the wine. The Aegean islands dominated the Levantine market till the day when the liberated Bulgars, aided by the French, replanted the famous vineyards of Thrace.

In this gloomy picture of Islamic grape growing a touch of color is furnished by the little urban vineyards of western Algeria. There in the neighborhood of the principal cities of the mountainous interior (such as Mascara and Miliana) one might find, long before the French occupation, genuine vineyards, with the plants ranged properly in order, and private wineries belonging to individual citizens. The mingling of strains, generally exotic ones, gave them a rather special bouquet, almost riotous in its richness, but there was a quality about them which was altogether extraordinary in Islamic countries, something inherited from Rome and the Andalusian tradition but reconstituted under the aegis of Islam after the destruction of the wine trade under the Arab invasions. (To be sure the Arabs had treated

vines no worse than they did other fruit-bearing plants.)
These were wines of a new atmosphere, quite different
from those of the great domains of antiquity. But they
were far from adequate to quench even the local thirst
of the Barbary Coast, where, in defiance of religious law,
renegades and pirates drank generously from stocks of
wine imported from Spain, Italy, and Provence.

A second interesting circumstance is the recent revival
of vine growing in Asia Minor. During the last years of
the Ottoman Empire the industry was essentially a concern of the fiscal office, which was preoccupied with
increasing the yield of the tax on alcohol and therefore
lent its influence to reconstituting vineyards in several
Christian villages. After the war of independence and
the expulsion of the Greeks the Turkish immigrants who
replaced them either neglected the vineyards or uprooted
the vines. But the government did not wish to be de-
prived of substantial revenues and so intervened. For
the first time in an Islamic country the state itself turned
vintner; the new immigrants did not make wine themselves but grew grapes which they sold to the state
liquor monopoly, which completed the process. The end
product was exported, chiefly to Scandinavian countries;
local consumption remained very slight. Today the winegrowing industry of Anatolia is completely artificial; it
produces only for sale and has no roots in the peasantry's
way of life or civilization; it is actually a relic.

The Islamic ban on other alcoholic drinks, other
stimulants, and narcotics has had less influence on agriculture and soil use than the ban on wine. For one thing
the ban is far from universally observed. The tolerance

shown by the Hanafites has greatly encouraged the drinking of *raki* ("brandy") in the whole of the eastern Mediterranean. This is the main form in which alcohol is consumed in Turkey. The map drawn up by E. Tumertekin shows clearly, however, that the use of alcohol is limited almost exclusively to the cities and the richest areas of the Aegean regions. The world of rural Anatolia is hardly touched at all. Elsewhere it is primarily at the frontiers of Islam that the ban on alcohol loses its force. Among the Moslems of Madagascar the use of fermented drinks, particularly of rum, is general. The greatest tolerance prevails among Chinese Moslems. In Black Africa, Islam has often found the ban on alcohol an obstacle to its expansion and has been able to make headway among the black populations only by softening its restrictions in this matter. In order to convert the Serer, who were fond of alcoholic drinks, the Mourid sheiks of Senegal did not hesitate to grant them dispensations for gin and juniper spirits. The Senussi have not been able to stop the Ouadai from drinking beer made of millet. At Djenné on the Niger, Moslems drink freely of ciders of low alcoholic content made from the fruits of the countryside. All along the line of Islamic advance in Africa palm wine and millet beer remain in general use. Among the Diulas, Moslem merchants are even active in distributing absinthe, gin, and cheap trading whiskey throughout the forests of the Ivory Coast. This relaxation of the rules extends even to certain men of God, who are jestingly known in the French district of Black Africa as "brandy" priests. Yet in a general way the rules against alcohol are enforced more strictly as time passes after a district's original conversion to Islam. Recent observers have noted progress of this sort in Senegal.

In Guinea the Moslems are more and more replacing alcohol with kola, which they use to excess. The Moslem who dies swollen up with kola is thought to go directly to Paradise after his death.

The ban on opium does not weigh much more heavily than that on alcohol. It is true that Moslem Chinese are less addicted to opium than the rest of their countrymen and are less apt to surrender to the drug. But countries like Iran and to a lesser degree Turkey are great centers of opium manufacture and consumption, and poppy growing is an important factor in the agricultural system. The ban on tobacco by the Wahhabi and Senussi has greatly reduced the amount of this crop grown in territory controlled by the latter sect, notably in Tripolitania, since the nineteenth century. But this prohibition remains strictly local; the ban on coffee by the Senussi (it does not extend to tea), has had no effect on the growing of coffee trees since these regions were not naturally suited to them. In Yemen the mystics held coffee in high esteem.

Forbidden foods and their consequences: (b) Illicit varieties of meat. Much more important in its consequences has been Islam's ban on pork, an old Near Eastern custom followed by Egyptians, Semites, and Libyans, and transmitted by them to Islam. It is a rule much better observed in Islamic countries than the rule against alcoholic beverages. Here again the exceptions to the rule are found on the frontiers of Islam. The clearest example of frontier tolerance is furnished by the Far East. In Indonesia, where conversion to Islam is often superficial, the tolerance of swine's flesh is universal. In China the greatest possible indulgence is common. Appearances are saved by the simple process of christening the pork "mutton." This hypocrisy is very general elsewhere, if one believes the proverb according to which "a Moslem traveling alone gets fat, two Moslems traveling together get thin" (because the solitary traveler does not scruple to eat pork when he is out of sight of his coreligionists). Another proverb declares, even more sharply, "One Moslem is no Moslem; two Moslems are half a Moslem; three Moslems are one Moslem." In Moslem lodginghouses and hotels pork is almost always served to non-Moslems. Yet the ban is better observed in Szechwan and generally in the western provinces. In Madagascar it is not followed at all. Certain clans abstain from pork, but they do so because of a local *fady* ("taboo") that has nothing to do with Islam. In Black Africa various adjustments to the ban have been worked out. The Senegalese sometimes consider the wart hog as an animal outside the pig family.

However, the ban on pork, like that on alcohol, is making progress. Several tribes which used to eat ass's flesh have given it up on purely philological grounds; the same word in their language (*m'bam*) designates both ass and pig. In certain Balkan areas where Islam had long been established, feeling in the matter reached a point where it influenced the Christians, some of whom refused to eat pork. Aside from these exceptions on the borders of Islam the only peoples who eat pork within the zone of Islam's influence are primitive tribes, half converted and considered impure. What is more, they are always hunters, and the problem centers on their eating of wild hogs, not domestic swine. Thus the Wayto, a caste of Moslem hunters using the Amharic tongue and living on the banks of the Blue Nile and Lake Tana, eat the flesh of the hippopotamus, which is impure for Moslems just as is pork. Among the Somali the Midgan caste of serfs and hunters eat any meat they like. The same is true of the Nimadi in Mauritania, of the Sahel people in the Sudan, and of the Hodh, who inhabit the region of Kiffa-Tichitt—savage, half-starved hunters, who adhere to Islam in name but eat all sorts of forbidden foods, above all the flesh of the wild boar. And yet the people of Kiffa feel obliged to seek an excuse for this behavior; tradition says it is due to the peaceful disposition of a pious warrior who preferred to eat forbidden meats rather than to raid the herds of his fellow Moslems. At Fouta Djallon, though the Fulah maintain strict dietary laws, their captives of whatever origin, for example the Malinke and the Dialonke, eat boar's flesh without shame. Outside of these primitive tribes or inferior castes, one can cite only certain Shiite heretics of the Near East, the Ahl-i-Hakks of Kurdistan and perhaps the Tahtadjis of Anatolia, whom the Sunnites charge with now and then eating boar's flesh, though they themselves deny it. But the Yazidi, though otherwise largely alienated from Islam, observe the ban. The Ghomara, Riffian heretics of the Middle Ages, permitted the flesh of female pigs and boars to be eaten.

The geographical effects of this ban on pork have been

considerable. The rule against pork has thrown open the wooded ranges to sheep and goats and thus indirectly brought about a catastrophic deforestation. This is one of the basic reasons for the sparse landscape particularly evident in the Mediterranean districts of Islamic countries. On the borders of Moslem rule, in Albania, for example, the amount of wooded countryside becomes much greater immediately one crosses into the Christian cantons, where pork is raised.

Islam has also made its contribution to a decrease in the practice of cynophagy, or dog eating, which is an old Libyan and Berber custom. The dog was a domestic animal of the ancient Libyans and was deliberately cultivated as food; it is still part of the alimentary picture in a broad zone of the Sahara reaching from North Africa (above all Derna in Tripolitania, Sfax in Tunisia, Gabès in the Fezzan, Chott Djerid, Souf, Touat, and Mzab) as far as Bahrein in the Orient. Dog's flesh is eaten not only in case of famine but also as a remedy against fever and as a fattening diet (the dogs are first stuffed with dates). Especially at Djerba is this diet customary for young ladies who wish to acquire the

ed by their future husbands.
em to tolerate the practice,
e eating of dog's flesh. The
n the fact that the animal is
rity of the Nimadi is linked
se professional hunters live in
logs) as well as from the fact
the dog enjoys a certain con-
uced the prevalence of this

typically Saharan custom, so that today it is scarcely more than a curiosity. On another level Islam rebukes the possessor of dogs that do not have an obvious practical value (as watchdogs, hunters, or progenitors of improved breeds [5]), and in this way it has considerably reduced the number of dogs kept for pleasure and for display.

The relations of Islam with the working of the soil. With respect to the positive influences of Islam on the working of the soil, the most obvious influence is certainly in the realm of the sheepherder. Says the Koran: "It is equally glorious to lead the flocks to their fold or into the pastures" (XVI, 6). Carried as it was by nomads or by sheep-raising peoples, Islam has spread its favored animal species across entire continents and in the wake of its conquests has converted great areas from crops to pasture. The spread of nomadism across cultivable plains, reinforced by the aversion of Islam to pork and by the sacred character of the sheep in Islam (every Moslem must sacrifice a goat, sheep, or other animal when he makes his pilgrimage and another each year at the sacrificial feast which marks the ending of Ramadan), accounts for the density of sheep in Islamic countries, and of their companions the goats as well; and to these close grazers the upland forests have been sacrificed. In China the Moslems have a practical monopoly of the sheep-growing trade. The Islamic conquests introduced new strains of sheep into Spain from North Africa.

The camel, which the Koran several times describes as a miraculous animal, was also introduced into new lands

[5] Bukhari, *op. cit.,* 3.

by the Islamic invaders, notably into Spain, where it had been seen only rarely before the Moslems came. (Its spread through North Africa is known to antedate the arrival of Islam.) The Byzantine defeat of the Arabs at the edge of the high Anatolian plateau is largely explained by Arab inability to accustom their camels to the cold winters of the high plateau. The only animals that could stand such cold were those of mixed blood, offspring of the Bactrian camels, which Anatolia had known since antiquity and which the Turks used there before bringing them into the Balkans and making use of them on Cyprus. It was as camel drivers, and secondarily as shepherds, that certain Moslems (Afghans and Beluchis, mostly) were brought to Australia, where their only predecessors were Malay sailors and pearl fishers who had lived along the coasts.

The Moslem is always a natural horseman. So it is in the Balkans, where the Bosnian Moslems have always prided themselves on their Arabian horses and looked down on their Christian neighbors. This horsemanship is not a simple function of social superiority, for many Chinese Moslems are breeders, sellers, and at need stealers or receivers of stolen horses (and thus often in a small way bandits). On the Camargue it is customary to attribute the fine breed of local horses to certain lucky crossbreedings made in Saracen times.

Finally, these animal raisers have also had an influence on the spread of large cattle. In China they raise beef cattle and have a practical monopoly of the trade. In Black Africa cattle raisers converted to Islam and descending from the north, like the Fulah, have had considerable influence on the raising of cattle in the central zones of Africa. Islamized traders, the Diulas, spread the practice of raising cattle through the great forest districts of the Ivory Coast, thus contributing, even before colonization took place, to the decline of cannibalism.

In the realm of agriculture proper one would expect the role of Islam to be much more modest; yet it is apparent in many circumstances. Islam has probably served most plainly as an instrument of agricultural progress in Black Africa, where it faced clearly inferior civilizations. Marty has emphasized the helpful role of Islam in the upper Ivory Coast. Although the Moslems there are mostly traders, their fields, when they have any, are better cultivated than those of their fetishist neighbors of the same race (Malinkés). They grow grains (rice and corn, millet and *fonio*, a cereal) in preference to yams and grow them more skillfully; their techniques are better, their hoes (*daba*) are stronger and wider, therefore heavier; they reap their rice with a sickle whereas among the fetishists the rice is picked a stalk at a time. The Diulas have developed the growing of cotton and have learned how to spin and weave it to meet Moslem clothing needs. Other Diulas, originally Fulah, who came from Masina, have succeeded in spreading the palm tree to the southern part of the Ivory Coast. Elsewhere (as in Niger), one observes the development by Islam of northern cereals, like wheat.

More than this Moslem cultures reveal a discipline in work and a unity of method that one does not generally find among the animists. The rural Moslem family makes its *lougans* ("temporary fields") one after the other.

Understandings between neighbors are the rule, and the Moslem families, which are more solidly organized than non-Moslem ones, work better under the authority of the head of the family. This order contrasts with the anarchy of the fetishists, and Marty has asserted that Islam, a force for stability and order, is at bottom hostile to an itinerant, a nomad, culture. And yet this superiority in agriculture is not decisive, for the farmer's life reacts on the Islamic beliefs of the new cultivators. Delafosse cites examples of Sarakole, city dwellers from north of the circle of Bamako (from the villages of Banamba, Kita, Kérouané), who were ruined by the decline of horse trading and the freeing of their slaves and so had to return to working in the fields; they abandoned Islam almost immediately for animism. Under such circumstances devotion to Islam cools or is entirely forgotten; every Moslem who returns to the soil seems lost to Islam.

On its northern frontier Islam with its pastoral, nomadic, and warfaring way of life has contributed almost nothing to agricultural life. The buckwheat, to be sure, despite its French name of *sarrasin* ("Saracen"), spread from central and eastern Asia only in the wake of the Mongol invasions. There is perhaps justification for the fact that in Provence the art of exploiting the cork oak and extracting pitch from the maritime pine tree is attributed to the Arabs. The most notable exception is Spain, where historians can explore to their hearts' content Islamic skill at crossing cultures and techniques. As for plants Islam, thanks to the constant stirring up provided by pilgrimages and inter-Islamic trade routes, was able to bring to Spain a multitude of Indian, Far Eastern, and tropical plants, which were unknown to or neglected by the Greeks—rice, sugar cane, indigo, saffron, henna, cotton, plums, the Syrian apricot (carried to Sicily and Andalusia), artichokes, and spinach.

As far as techniques are concerned, there is a problem concerning Arabian influence on irrigation in Spain. The Arabs, it seems, introduced there the cultivation of orchards and gardens, as well as the old Egyptian-Chaldean techniques of irrigation. The Spanish language includes many Arabian terms in its technical vocabulary for irrigation; for example, *noria* ("water wheel"). But are we really dealing here with an Arabian invention, or even with an original introduction of the Arabs? The irrigation of crops was practiced on a major scale in the eastern Mediterranean, was it not, long before the Arabs? Nonetheless it is probable that they brought about decisive advances. The question of water wheels has been summarized by L. Torres-Balbas, who observes the similarity of Spanish and Moroccan *norias* with those of the Near East and concludes that the Arabs introduced certain improvements on Asiatic techniques that were invented in the Orient at a very early period. In fact, the techniques and customs of irrigation in the Near East are clearly pre-Islamic. There too Islam was a propagator rather than a creator. It seems that even the Mongols learned the techniques of irrigation from the Moslems. Islamic legislation on the subject of water is very liberal and favorable to the rights of private property, once the precept of charity is satisfied with regard to drinking water.

On a more general plane the proscription of pork has driven Moslems to seek in the world of vegetables for their principal sources of fats; they have cultivated sesame, peanuts (developed in Senegal by the Mourid sect—see below), and above all the olive tree. For special reasons this seems a typically Islamic tree. It produces light for the sanctuaries; and Mohammed himself calls it a blessed tree. Its cultivation is carried on everywhere in the neighborhood of the mosques (in the same way that the churches and convents of Christianity lent themselves to the culture of the vine). It was ignored by the Nabataeans, predecessors of the Arabs, and by the Arabs themselves until the arrival of Islam. At that time they acquired the olive tree from the Aramaeans (the Arabic name for olive tree, *zeitoun*, is of Aramaean origin), undoubtedly to meet the needs of their creed and their liturgy, which was strongly influenced by Byzantine Christianity. Yet the fact that Islam was usually spread by nomads generally resulted, at least in the first stages of conquest, in the destruction of the olive groves. In North Africa the groves diminished markedly after the Islamic conquest as compared with their numbers before the Hilal invasions, and they decreased in Sicily also. An isolated circumstance was that the Yazidis of Mount Sanjar continued to derive the oil of their sanctuaries from sesame, so that a little island of sesame culture was maintained in this area, although a rigorous ban was imposed on the production of certain vegetables, such as cabbage, beans, and lettuce.

Trades and crafts in Islam. More than sheep raising, even more than landlordism, trade and craftsmanship are the noblest and most meritorious activities of a Moslem. It is as traders and craftsmen primarily that Moslems penetrate non-Islamic countries. Trade and crafts characterize the Moslem minorities beyond the frontiers of Islam and constitute the most tangible mark of its advance.

In China, except for the great communities of the northwest and southwest which include some farmers, most of the Moslems are composed of traders, artisans, and transport workers (this last occupation is probably linked to their gift for horse breeding; G. Cordier has shown that there is no great proportion of Moslems among the mule-driving caravanners of Yunnan). They control the trade in tea throughout a whole district of Szechwan, and sometimes the trade in silk and cotton as well. Working in hides, pottery, and jade and money changing are their principal occupations. Many keep hotels; others are in charge of public baths (*hammams*). In Tibet and also in Lhasa the urban Moslem minority is composed essentially of tradesmen. Moslems are also found in the commercial posts on the caravan routes, beside the great Buddhist monasteries. In Buddhist countries where there are religious laws against the shedding of blood they often become butchers; for example, certain Afghan Moslems have become butchers in Cambodia. All the butchers of Lhasa are Chinese Moslems of the Hui-Hui, originally from the province of Koko Nor (Tsinghai). The same situation prevails in Black Africa. On the frontiers of Islam this Moslem turning to butchering as a trade must certainly be linked with the need to maintain ritual precautions with regard to the slaughter of animals. It is all the more remarkable because in Arabian and Berber countries butchering is much scorned. (In Kabylia only the Akli, black or half-breed descendants of slaves, can be butchers; in Algeria it is often the Homria, offspring of Mzabite men and Negro women, who form a separate caste at Ghardaïa and act in Algiers as butchers or scavengers.) Starting as butchers, they often become cattle merchants. In Cambodia the Moslem town of Prek Pra, less than 10 kilometers from Pnompenh, has a nationwide monopoly on traffic in cattle, either for sale to butchers in the towns or for export via Saigon. In southern and southeastern Asia Moslem towns are essentially concerned with trade and ocean travel. The Moslem minorities of French Indochina, the Chams of southern Annam, Cochin China, and Cambodia, are composed mainly of fishers and transport workers, living in worm-shaped villages along the water courses and seashores and trading in rice, tobacco, and wood, out of which they make their log canoes. Farming communities are relatively infrequent in these parts.

In southern India the Moslem Labbays of the Coromandel Coast are a caste of sailors, fishers, and tradesmen, who make nets and sell salt fish; sometimes they grow and sell the betel nut. They trade in hides and do some hunting (with arrows darted from bamboo tubes). In the same region the Marecars are an exclusive caste of tradesmen, sailors, and armorers. The Moplahs of the Malabar Coast, of mixed Arabian and Dravidian blood, cultivate some land in the interior at the same time that they carry on trade, but they prefer the second occupation. They are often grocers, and sometimes work in leather, binding books and making saddles. They have a monopoly on making oil from a reed known as camel's hay, which they buy and cut in the forests. When poor, they naturally become coolies and take to work on the railroads. Elsewhere castes of Moslem peddlers and merchants like the Khodjas and the Shiite Bohoras of Gujarat or the Sunnite Memans of Kathiawar are widely diffused and very active. Generally the proportion of Moslem communities devoted to trade or handicrafts is particularly high in countries where the majority of the population is Hindu. Indian penetration into eastern and central Africa was often accomplished primarily through these Moslem traders and peddlers. On the island of Mauritius, where Indians were formerly in a majority, the Moslems now have practically a monopoly of the trade in grains and cloth. The characteristic handicraft worker and trader recur in the European Moslem minorities.

In the Balkans most of the Moslems inhabit towns. In Bosnia they are in a majority in certain occupations, such as shoemakers and tailors, leatherworkers and tanners, makers of riding saddles and packsaddles, gold- and silversmiths, cutlers, and, more prosaically, barbers and bakers. In Finland the few hundred Tartars who constitute the Moslem minority occupy an important position in the fur trade.

This emphasis on trade is particularly marked in Black Africa. The Ethiopian Moslems, the Jabarti, whose villages are scattered over the heights of Shoa, where they constitute the remnants of the Moslem invasion of the sixteenth century, include a number of farmers but are mostly composed of tradesmen and artisans. In all the eastern part of Black Africa the trading Mande-Diulas, the Hausas and Nagos, and the Dendi of upper Dahomey control the commercial life of the deep forests far beyond the frontiers of Islam itself. Every pagan who takes part in this itinerant commerce is gained, almost automatically, by Islam. Even Christians from Syria and Lebanon, who are numerous among the peddlers of eastern Africa, distribute Islamic amulets and pass themselves off as Moslems in order to gain prestige and attract more clients. In the country of Bambara, a center of resistence to Islam, the Somonos, a caste of fishermen and boatmen who are scattered along the Niger and are vassals of the Bambara, constitute one of the few groups professing Islam. Similiarly the greater part of the handicraft work produced in the zone of deep forests is done by Moslems (weaving, dyeing, tanning, leather- and metalwork). On the lower Ivory Coast woodcutters are recruited from the Moslems—Fanti and Apollonians, originally from the Gold Coast. The only obstacle to the progress of Islam among the artisans of Black Africa is the existence of specialized castes in the traditional social structure of the fetishists. Thus at Fouta Djallon, Islam collided head-on with the strongest prejudices of custom and social hierarchy, handicraft work being traditionally servile and proper only to inferior castes and slaves. Under these circumstances trade is the only acceptable outlet for the Diulas. In Senegal the activity of the Moorish *m'allem*, or "master," who works in ebony to make jewels, beads, and little decorated boards in which to bind the Koran, is strictly confined to one side of the river; on the left bank, the Laobes, a fetishist caste of carpenters, have a monopoly on woodworking. The same sort of obstacles exist in India, and on an even larger scale.

THE GEOGRAPHY OF PILGRIMAGES IN ISLAM

Being, as it is, a tradesman's religion, Islam has encouraged in still another way the mixing together of men and objects. Christianity has its own special pilgrimages, but even the pilgrimage to Jerusalem is far from being all-important in the religious life of the West. But in Islam the pilgrimage to Mecca is an absolute commandment, which has many consequences for the unity of the Islamic world; it establishes a single web of social, religious, and commercial relations from the Atlantic Ocean to Indonesia. This great annual movement is one of the essential aspects of Islam's influence on geography. Although it is impossible to analyze in detail the routes taken by pilgrims near their countries of origin, a well-defined network of roads was quickly established on the Arabian Peninsula and in its immediate vicinity, subject naturally to occasional sudden variations and seizures of traffic.

There are three traditional methods of approach by land. The Egyptian caravan, starting at Cairo, began to move around the year 500 A.H. (A.D. 1106) through Asyut to El Quseir and Aidhab on the Red Sea, thence to Jidda. Another route ran through Suez, Aqaba, and Yenbo (this route was regularly organized in 809 A.H. (A.D. 1406/7). The Damascus caravan, created by the sultans in the middle of the thirteenth century, passed through Ma'an and Medina. The Persian caravan, departing from Kermanshah and Baghdad, alternated between two principal routes, that of Najaf-Hail-Medina or that of Samawa-Taif. It often joined forces with the caravan from Yemen, originating at Sana. This entire network is today reduced to the single route of the Yemen caravan and the local network of Hejaz villages. Since the first half of the ninteenth century, travel by land has steadily given way in the face of competition from steamboats plying the Red Sea and in consequence of the opening of the Suez Canal. Thus the number of Syrian pilgrims taking the trip via Hejaz declined from ten or twelve thousand in 1836 to three thousand in 1852–1853. After the great cholera epidemic of 1865 the establishment of an international sanitary control encouraged the persistence of land routes as a means of returning from the pilgrimage. Arriving generally by sea, the pilgrims generally chose to return by land whenever the pilgrimage was declared contaminated in order to avoid long and strict quarantines at the lazaretto of Tor in the Gulf of Suez. In effect, the length of the caravan journey served as an effectual quarantine. Thus by the end of the nineteenth century the number of people going to Mecca in the Syrian caravan declined to a few hundred, but the number of pilgrims returning by the same route might be as high as 15,000 (as in 1907) if the whole pilgrimage was declared contaminated. The same tendency occurred among the Persians. They came by sea, especially after 1868 (they were somewhat slower in abandoning the land routes), but many of them returned by land in order to visit Karbala and Najaf, cities whose attractions reinforced the influence of the sanitary regulations. At the same time the advent of steamship travel simplified the pilgrimage of the Indians, many of whom during the age of the sailing ships had had to wait at Medina or Mecca for the coming of the summer monsoons in order to get back home. It is estimated that at the end of the nineteenth century two thirds of the pilgrims coming from a distance arrived by sea. (Local pilgrims of Hejaz generally constitute at least one fourth or one third of the grand total.) In 1893, 47,000 people arrived by caravan (16,000 of them Yemenites) as against 94,000 by sea.

A new phase began with the construction of the Hejaz railway, undertaken by Abdul-Hamid in order to re-capture the great mass of Moslem pilgrims from the foreign steamship companies. The line was completed to Medina in 1908. Pilgrims returning by train out-numbered those arriving that way for the same old reason—to escape quarantine (in 1912 there were 19,000 returnees as against 8,000 arrivals). After the First World War the railroad failed to resume operations. Attempts to revive the old land routes through the use of caravans in order to avoid the expense of passports also failed of success, and in 1933–1935 there were no more than a few hundred pilgrims who arrived by caravan. An auto-mobile road from Baghdad to Medina also remained a curiosity. The latest development is the advent of air transportation (in 1950, 11,500 pilgrims came by air out of a grand total of 95,000).

The total number of pilgrims is subject to variation as spectacular as the variation in methods of travel. The pilgrimage reached its height in 1912 with 300,000 pilgrims (there were 225,000 in 1927). Reduced by the wars (there were only 23,000 in 1941), the pilgrimage has also been much affected by economic conditions, notably when the pilgrims come from a distant land but also whenever their native land is economically hard hit. Between 1928 and 1933 the great depression brought about a diminution in the number of pilgrims arriving by sea from 97,000 to 20,000. Arrivals from British India over this period were relatively more stable (declining from 13,000 to 7,000) than those from the Netherlands Indies (who declined from 49,000 to a mere 2,000), probably because the depression had greater effects on a plantation economy (the price of rubber was much reduced) rather than because of the distance which the pilgrims had to come, for during this same period the number of Egyptian arrivals also declined from 14,000 to 1,500. The pilgrimage to Mecca is thus marked by the same instability that characterizes the entire human geography of the Near East. Nonetheless its effects have been considerable, and the pilgrims have carried away with them many new customs, devices, and even seedlings of plants (for example, the rubber tree was brought in this way to Southeast Asia).

Aside from the pilgrimage to Mecca, moreover, Islamic countries have a whole network of local pilgrimages, linked chiefly to the worship of the saints and to the brotherhoods, and hence, it would seem, more widely expanded in the Islamic Maghreb than in the Near East but still to be found everywhere. There seems to be no general rule governing the sites to which these pilgrimages are addressed; they may be urban or rural, of human construction (sanctuaries) or natural (grottoes, mountains, and so forth), and very often they are of pre-Islamic origin. Some of these pilgrimages bring together every year several hundred thousand people. In 1937 some 250,000 pilgrims gathered at the tomb of Ahmed Bamba, founder of Mouridism, at Touba (Baol) in Senegal; several hundred thousand observed the anniversary of Sidi Ahmed el-Badawi at Tanta in the Nile Delta; nearly 100,000 were in Algeria at Inkermann at the shrine of Sidi Abed, to cite only a few examples. If it were possible to draw up a map showing the number of pilgrims throughout Islam, it might contain a number of surprises. E. Dermenghem has observed on the high plateaus near Oran, as well as in the upland plains of eastern Tell, the part played by local pilgrimages in bringing about vast assemblies of nomad tribes. In general, the function of the Islamic pilgrimage seems indissolubly linked to its role in the economic relations of the people.

The Shiite pilgrimages merit special mention because of the importance of the human currents which they set in motion. In Iraq the cities of Karbala and Najaf, Samarra and Qazimain, draw crowds of Iranian pilgrims toward the shrines of the martyr Husein. But also, more remarkably, these cities attract corpses, which are brought there to be buried in sacred ground. In 1932 it was estimated that nearly 200,000(?) corpses were imported into Iraq, for the most part by caravan and under extremely insanitary conditions. There was even an airline that ran from Isfahan to Karbala for the purpose of carrying dead bodies, and it was the only Iranian airline that was able to function without government support. Finally, the Iranian government closed its frontiers and turned the flood of bodies toward the holy Iranian cities of Qum and Meshed.

CHAPTER II

Groupings and Modes of Life
Derived from Religion
in the Countries of Islam

Modes of life derived from religion in Islam: The Maraboutic ("saintly") tribes. Up to this point we have considered Islam as a unit, making note of its principal outward manifestations. The following paragraphs will attempt to analyze its internal differentiations. To what degree does the particularly strict observance of its precepts influence human life, what is the effect of heretical deviations, and what is the geographical division of different groups?

So far as the effects of a deepened religious life are concerned, it has been said (by P. Deffontaines) that Islam properly speaking does not have any distinct variations in religious modes of life. Certainly it has no clearly distinguished clergy, no true priestly class. Yet it is plainly unrealistic to pretend that monasticism does not exist in Islam, that its place has been taken by the holy war. Disregarding for the moment the unorthodox sects, of which we will talk later, the communities of dervishes that are scattered throughout the Near East and certain brotherhoods of Islamic North Africa set themselves clearly apart from the general order of life. It was the same with the whirling dervishes of Turkey, the Mevlevis, a brotherhood of workers and artists, many of whom were jewelers or manufacturers of *objets d'art*. In Morocco, in the Zerhoun, certain brotherhoods which profess rites of blood, such as the Hamadcha and the Dghoughiyyin are set off professionally and ethnically and are continually expanding among colored people in humble occupations such as smiths, butchers, and shoemakers. And certainly those nomadic dervishes, the mendicant Kalenders, who swarm on the very verges of orthodoxy throughout the Near East, have an individual and peculiar way of life. In the days of the Ottoman conquest monastic houses of dervishes often played a sizable role. Communities of colonizing dervishes were notable for cultivating the land, growing fruit trees (plums) and rosebushes. They were situated, by preference, in countries newly opened to colonization, among the mountains or along the great arteries of traffic. In general, however, all these examples serve merely to suggest exceptions to a rule. The Islamic brotherhood has rarely had a specific geographical base, and its expansion is generally bound up with the accidents of individual proselytizing.

But the most notable differentiation is that of the Maraboutic ("saintly") tribes. This is the name given throughout the Sahara (in Mauritania they bear the name of Tolbas or of Zawaiyas) to certain nomad tribes which carry no arms but give themselves up to prayer and study. Their legendary origin is generally sought in some pious personage who, weary of brigandage and eager to return to God, exercised a moderating influence on his tribe and caused it to give up the practices of raiding and pillaging to which the warrior tribes (*hassanis* in Mauritania) continued to devote themselves. All sorts of stages exist between warlike and Maraboutic tribes, since a number of the latter can cease to be Maraboutic when a favorable occasion offers, others carry arms for purposes of self-defense, and still others are very handy warriors. They are sometimes simply men of easy circumstances whose wealth and good fortune have rendered them indifferent to the temptations of anarchy and pillage and who have no interest in anything but peace and security. But the typical Maraboutic tribe is a disarmed, and a vassal tribe, paying tribute to its warrior tribe in return for protection and furnishing it with chaplains, men of letters, and clerks, thereby relieving the master tribe of all its spiritual concerns even to the fasting required during the month of Ramadan.

Aside from these ultimately subordinate activities and the practice of making amulets and rosaries the Maraboutic tribes have a wholly different life basis from the warrior tribes. Pacificism and devotion, as they eliminate the exceptional resources furnished by war, provide occasion for a material life much more intense and better organized than the warrior tribes can undertake. Unlike the warrior tribes, which are great camel drivers, cut off from the soil, and very much at home wherever they pitch their tents, the "saintly" tribes are often half-agricultural, half-pastoral; the areas which they control are always well defined. In Senegal and Mauritania they have been primarily devoted for the last two centuries to extracting and collecting gum arabic from acacia trees, a pursuit which has no appeal for the warrior tribes. Collecting gum is carried on far to the south in Black Africa, and there these pious folk find opportunities to convert the natives—opportunities which have had a profound effect in strengthening Islam in the Ouolof country.

Their trade in gum arabic occasioned early contacts with the French. These "saintly" tribes devoted to order and peace and frequently bullied by the warrior tribes have been responsive to colonization, perhaps as a reaction against the insecurity fostered by the great nomadic peoples. Far from cultivating fanaticism or hostility to foreigners, they have almost always supported the extension of French power. Furthermore they have attempted to profit by new conditions. J. Chaumeil describes a Maraboutic tribe of the Anti-Atlas district, the Ait Abdallah or Said (they inhabit the plain of Ilerh and part of the limestone plateau of Agadir Izir—near Tafraout). They consist of refugees from many different countries, discredited in their own tribes and incapable of living a warrior's life; they are treated condescendingly by the other tribes of the district, serving as preachers, healers, and mediators on any mission that is slightly humiliating. They are scarcely considered free men and are restricted to a very secondary position in traditional society. Since the colonial pacification, they have tried to profit by their knowledge of Islamic law to fill out their patrimony and have launched a number of legal actions against their neighbors, with documents drawn up full and fair. But very little has actually been done to improve their status. They are not prepared to fight for their existence, nor to emigrate to the great world outside the Anti-Atlas, and their level of life has risen but slightly. Religion still takes first place, and the weight of tradition remains heavy.

General conditions of religious segregation in Islamic countries. Just as segregation is the rule in Islamic towns, so ethnic and religious segregation is universally present in the Moslem countryside. The notion of a minority, geographically united and spiritually coherent, is one of the basic principles in reconciling populations to living together. The ideological foundations for this state of things have been clearly defined on the religious level by B. Lewis. The principal criterion is maintenance of political order. Heresy, which is a struggle between popular piety and dogmatic religion, has no religious base when it is faced with an orthodoxy enlarged beyond all measure. Thus it becomes defined essentially as a refusal to accept the existing order, as subversion, as attacks upon the state, the dynasty, and society in general. Under these conditions every heretical sect is bound to separate itself as much as possible from the central authority. In Islam every heretic is a refugee under someone's power. Not one of them would be able to live close to a monarch. This means that the distribution of heresies is primarily rural. These turbulent communities install themselves in districts far removed from the centers of urban power. There they discover elements anterior to Islam which have survived by passive resistance far from the most dynamic centers of expanding faith and Arabization, which are found in the cities; primarily they find in the country the various Christian sects. In the areas around the cities the Moslem countryside looks like a jig-saw puzzle, a mosaic of ethnic and religious groups.

The preceding analysis, though it describes the fundamental rules of Islamic development, will not serve for the entire Islamic world. There are regions and areas where one finds an abundance of sects and minorities, where the religious map, seen in conjunction with the details of geographical conditions, presents an impression of prodigious multiplicity. There are also vast areas where the faith of Sunnite Islam prevails unbroken. A simple glance at the polychrome map of Moslems in the world, edited by the Centre des Hautes Etudes d'Administration musulmane in 1952, enables one to distinguish these two groups of countries clearly. The land marked by religious complexity and segregation extends from Anatolia to India, from the Caucasus to Arabia. Broadly speaking it is the Near East. Elsewhere, North Africa, Black Africa, and Southeast Asia are, with rare exceptions, districts dominated by orthodox uniformity. The reasons for this contrast of regions are evident. The land with many sects and segregation is that on which Islam has most clearly placed its stamp and which is at the same time a remarkable crossroads of trade and invasion routes. It is a land naturally fertile in religions and prophets, where tribal and national differences, strongly based on differences of geography, have naturally taken

a religious form at the same time that the intense working of the Islamic creed has released innumerable reac-
tions. The countries of universal orthodoxy are, on the
other hand, countries where Islam is more relaxed, where
the imprint of the religion is often more recent and
almost always weaker, and where there survive under
the cover of superficial Islamic belief many traditional
traits. Beneath a very recent and halfhearted Islamic influence there persists a subsoil that has not had to seek
an escape from the rigors of orthodox discipline in the
development of heresy. Indigenous religious feeling here
finds expression primarily in the brotherhoods. While
special modes of life and of religious segregation flourish
in the Near East, a region *makhzen* ("of strict government control") by its very nature, they are largely absent
from regions of dissidence such as North Africa. There
the pre-Islamic Berber social organization persists amid
the great mountain ranges, and political autonomy of
this sort plays the same role as does heresy in the Near
East. The mountain refuges, which are religious in the
Near East, are ethnic and linguistic in North Africa.

Types of segregation. (*a*) *Mountain refuges.* Mountain
ranges are in fact the primary religious refuges in Islamic
countries. Throughout the Near East they are set apart
from the flat land and the great trade routes, which are
given up generally to Sunnite Islam. The mountains are
so many breeding places of heterodoxy. This fact is
clearest in the Fertile Crescent. Thus the Maronite
Christians have their center in northern Lebanon, in the
most rugged mountains, where springs and, formerly,
forests were most frequent and whence they could

spread into the outskirts of the Kura district and along the coast. Mingling progressively with the Druses toward the south and diminishing proportionately in numbers, they become relatively more numerous in the last mountainous spurs of central Lebanon. Completely missing from northern Lebanon, the Druses appear to the south of Nahr-el-Kelb, as far as a line drawn between Damur and Jezzin, in the regions of the Meten and the Shuf, where they are closely mixed with the Christians. But their main center since the migrations that followed the wars of the eighteenth century has been in the basaltic ridges of inner Syria, on what has become, because of them, Jebel Druze, or "Mountain of the Druses," and on Mount Hermon. The juncture with Lebanon is made through several villages scattered in the Bekaa, the valley between the Lebanon and Anti-Lebanon Mountains.

The Nusairi, whose doctrine was born in lower Iraq, occupied Mount Ansariye in northern Syria during the tenth century and have been complete masters of this area since the fourteenth century, though the sect has disappeared elsewhere. The Alawite Mountains have remained their domain, where they live in total isolation, surrounded by hostile plainsmen, without any possible outlet to the sea. This explains their difference from the Maronites and the Druses, their stagnation as compared to the freedom of the Lebanese. Their economy remains very archaic, without plantations.

The Yazidis are also typical mountaineers, localized in the district of Shaikhan and above all on Mount Sinjar to the west of Mosul in Iraqi territory; in Turkey to the south of the Armenian mountains near Diyarbakir, Siirt, and Van; in Syria on Mount Siman (near the Turkish frontier south of Kilis) and in the upper Jezire (since the eighteenth century and after 1925 as refugees from Turkey); and in Iran at the village of Jabbarlu, near Tabriz. Unlike the Alawites, they are more specifically gardeners and planters than cultivators of grain, at least those from Mount Sinjar are; they were afraid to leave the mountains to raise grains on the plain.

The Ismaili are another example, even more characteristic if possible, of the refugee sect. There are several villages of them, perched like eagle's nests in upper Yemen on Mount Haraz. Though they could not maintain their foothold among the mountains on the Caspian side of the Iranian plateau (where they had their center at Alamut in the mountains of the Rhoudbar, not far from Kazvin), they did manage to subsist in Syria in castles hidden away in the heart of the Alawite range, which they shared with the sect of the same name. Others took refuge in the mountains of the middle basin of the Indus, around and upstream from the bend in the river (Hunza, Sirikol) and in the valleys of Pamir (Wakchan —upper valley of the Amu-Darya—and Badakhshan). From there they reached the Hindu Kush and spread through the oases of Turkestan, from Balkh to Bukhara.

In Arabia also differences in elevation are responsible for religious divisions. The Zaydites of Yemen occupy the high country, especially between Ibb and Sada, while the Sunnites occupy the coastal plain, the Tehama, and come in contact with the mountainous region only on the south. Contrasting with the low hollows of Hejaz, the land where Islam originated and where the sacred towns still stand, is the high country of Nejd, rocky and desertlike, always in opposition to the caliphs originating in Mecca, a classic land of heresy, where the Kharijite rebellions and the Karmathian insurrections were fomented, the place where Ismaili and crypto-Christians took refuge, and finally where the movement of Wahhabism found its center.

The religious geography of the Iranian plateau is no less characteristic. Although the upper plateau was unified by central authority within the framework of official Shiism, with its belief in the twelve descendants of Ali, the peripheral mountains escaped entirely. The distribution of the dissident Shiite sect of Ahl-i-Hakk is typical. It occupies the greater part of Luristan and has spread into the central Shiite section of Kurdistan. In Azerbaijan it is clearly limited to the mountainous districts, Sahend, Karaca Dag, and Soqqar Dag. Members of the sect are found on the Caspian slope, between Kazvin and Resht and in the area of Mount Demavend. There are, however, very few of them on the plateau proper (a few hamlets in the region of Hamadan and a few tribes of Turk-speaking nomads).

Sunnism is also strong in the peripheral regions, in Kurdistan and the Arabian lowlands of the south, in the coastal plains of the Caspian (Talech), or beyond the barriers of mountains. The mountains around the Caspian, a savage and wooded district, have always been a hotbed of revolts and heresies, a center of Ismaili activity, and an area into which Babism gladly expanded during the last century, when it promptly lost its fraternal and peace-loving character to become particularly violent and warlike.

To the east of the great desert of Lut (Dasht-i-Lut) and protected by it, Khurasan likewise has always played the role of a mountain refuge, for the Zoroastrians after the Islamic conquest, for the Kharijites later, and for the Ismaili, who are numerous there today. The greatest tolerance still prevails in this province, where one finds, besides Sunnites (Bujd near Birjand), a colony of Sikhs and a number of Babis.

On the other hand, the distribution of Anatolian Shiism, if one excepts the professional segregation of the Tahtadjis (see below), seems to have been much less influenced by geographical factors. Bektaschism in the cities and Alevism in the villages are the expressions of a sort of Turkish national reaction against the Arabic-Persian culture, and they have spread widely through the Turkmen nomads, many of whom for this reason sought out the Iranian land after Shiism became the official religion there. But they have generally concealed their existence under a protective hypocrisy and an apparent orthodoxy. The growth of Bektashism in the mountains of Albania is linked simply to military colonization and its absorption of neighboring populations. In Anatolia, though Shiism appears generally more prevalent the farther one advances to the east toward Iran, and also more diffused in the refuges provided by the Pontus and Taurus Mountain ranges, there are villages professing it on the high plateau itself, within a very short distance of the main roads.

Outside the Near East, segregation in the mountains is more limited, for reasons indicated above. In North Africa one can cite only isolated cases, the Zkaras of the mountains to the southwest of Ujda in Morocco, a number of whom migrated into Algeria in 1897, and some Berber-speaking Ibadites on Mount Nefusa in Tripolitania clinging to the rough ravines on the edge of the Saharan table, an island of mountaineering and tree-growing peasants in the middle of Arabianized Sunnite Bedouins—but in this last case having to resort to a type of refuge other than mountains, the desert.

b) *Refuges of the plain: sects of the desert and the oasis.* In the arid or semiarid zone which Islam occupies there is always another means of escaping the long arm of public law; one can flee to the desert, as men have done since ancient times and long before the coming of Islam. Flat land, even when it is not desert, may, if it is sufficiently out of the way of the great roads, accommodate a heretical sect. The example of the Metwalis of Lebanon is characteristic in this respect. Outside upper Galilee and the extreme south of Lebanon proper they have found a refuge in the north of Bekaa, that arid valley which has never served as a means of transportation, since north-south journeys are made along the coast or by way of the desert and east-west travelers generally go more to the south. Chased out of central Bekaa and the mountains of Lebanon, they found refuge here. In the same way swamps like those of lower Iraq have protected the Mandaeans (or Sabaeans) around Amara, Nasiriya, and Basra.

The desert, however, offers much grander possibilities.

The best example of a desert sect in North Africa is that of the Ibadites. E. F. Gautier has shown that Kharijism in its totality is a religion of the steppes and the upland pastoral plains; its base is Berber, democratic, and Zenata nomadic; it represents an antisocial reaction against urban civilization. After the destruction of the kingdom of Sijilmassa at Tafilalet and of the confederation of Tiaret, wanderings in the desert brought them to Ouargla, Mzab, and Siwa and finally caused them to gather together around Mount Nefusa. "There is scarcely an oasis, from Gabès to Figuig and Sijilmassa," says Masqueray, "which the Kharijites have not had a hand in developing. They have been the colonizers of the Sahara." They also persisted on the coast of Oman (at Muscat) beyond the Arabian desert, whence some of them wandered off toward Zanzibar, embarkation point of the Oman slave-trading fleet.

Other sects too have played a role in the creation of oases and the colonizing of the desert. When in 1855 the Senussi confederation moved its headquarters near to the wells of Jarabub, a caravan load of captured slaves was settled in the oasis to develop plantations and assure the life of the *zawiya* or "seat of the brotherhood." Another example of the desert refuge is provided by the communal sect of the Ghoudf in Mauritania (Tagant), composed of people drawn together from varied lands and of diverse castes, who were led to the desert by the desire to hold all their goods in common.

c) *Professional segregation in the countryside.* Can we say that this geographical division of heretical sects which we have characterized as "fortification" is reinforced by a professional specialization, by special ways of exploiting the soil? Country life, where the division of labor is not very marked, is not generally propitious to developments of this sort, and heretics or members of minority groups are rarely isolated in agricultural communities. Moreover the gathering of peasants into communities discourages the formation of a minority. Yet in certain areas such a formation has undoubtedly encouraged men to give themselves to particular occupations. Among the Indian Bohoras all the Shiites are traders, while a number of the Sunnites are farmers. Very curious is the specialization of the Anatolian Alevites in the Taurus, where they are known as Tahtadjis ("woodcutters"). They lead a nomadic life between the plains and the upland forests, where they have a monopoly on the use of wood, which has been entirely abandoned by the peasants. The origin of these Tahtadjis has been much discussed. The German anthropologist Von Luschan considers them a remnant from the most ancient ethnic stock of Asia Minor, the Armenoid race, brachycephalic and plano-occipital. Some Turkish ethnologists, on the other hand, consider them pure Turkmen nomads, fresh from the steppes of Central Asia, who provided a favorable field of Shiite propaganda. It is probable that we are here dealing with a mixture of several elements brought together for religious reasons, Shiism having been the defensive reaction of an older population settlement resulting from separatist tendencies among the nomad tribes. As for the professional specialty, it is a natural result of their fortifying themselves in the wooded uplands and of the fear of forests manifested by Sunnite peasants.

On the agricultural level, if one excepts Alawite and Yazidian agriculture, any original ideas on the part of the heretics seem very small indeed. And yet certain movements have encouraged the formation of agricultural establishments. Ibn Saud attempted to organize his ikhwan ("brethren" and soldiers) into rural colonies, and Wahhabism in general seems to have undertaken to settle nomads into fixed homes. The world of Black Africa, however, has the only sects or brotherhoods that can truly be called agrarian, primarily those of the Mourids of Ahmed Bamba in Senegal. The Mourid Serignes have created agricultural villages, which are easily recognized, by their square plans and staircases raised by a rope, as the work of practical men ready to go straight to their goal with no fear whatever of the malignant spirits that terrify the animists. They even build square huts, the corners of which might well conceal spirits hostile to living men. Outside of this remarkable disdain of superstition, which can be seen in the very appearance of their dwellings, Mouridism has been a major influence on the growing of the peanut in Senegal. Its expansion is linked to the improvement of the land around Cayor and Baol. It extends through a vast crescent to the west of the plains of Ferlo, between those plains and the railroad lines of Dakar to Thiès and Thiès to Kayes, with its lower point in eastern Salum. In the country of Balante (Casamance) the Fadeliya, a group of the Qadiriya, have also undertaken communal cultivation of millet, rice, and peanuts. In this attraction of the sects to agriculture there is something specific to Black Islam. We have already seen that a return to the land endangered Islam itself, and it is only on the margins of orthodoxy that this impulse to work the land has developed at all.

d) *Urban minorities.* In contrast to the heretical sects that have fortified themselves in mountainous refuges or in oases protected by the desert, there is also a very different attitude that leads a minority group to seek safety in economic and social activity, in its competitive abilities, in the opportunities for accumulation which are provided by cities. This attitude could not possibly be assumed, at least in traditional Islam, by heretical sects, which, as we have seen, are characterized by political subversion. It supposes that the group recognizes lawful authority and seeks protection from that authority. It is essentially the mark of non-Moslem minorities, at least of those ("peoples of the book") whose existence Islam admits. A whole group of them have deliberately chosen to endure the vexations that are the lot of an urban minority as a way of assuring their own prosperity, and to seek security not by taking refuge in more or less inaccessible places but by reaching an understanding with the established power.

The most perfect type of this minority is provided by a number of Christian communities in the Near East. Thus the Orthodox Greeks of Lebanon are essentially limited to the cities and their immediate environs around Beirut and Tripoli, as well as in the southern region of Bekaa around the road from Beirut to Damascus, where they are intimate neighbors of the Sunnite Moslems, a community which is also located in the big cities and along the main roads. Greek Catholics, whose eyes are more generally fixed on horizons outside Islam, are, on the other hand, much less markedly urban, and their affinity for town life is observed more especially in cities of the second order (such as Sidon, Tyre, and Zahle). At the same time a remnant of them may be found in the central section of southern Lebanon and at the eastern foot of the Anti-Lebanon.

In a general way throughout the Near East, Christian Arabs are particularly numerous in the cities; this is true in Palestine as well as in Syria (Damascus) or in Iraq (Baghdad). Outside upper Egypt the Egyptian Copts appear in great numbers only in the main cities, notably in Old Cairo. The Mandaeans of Iraq possess communities in the cities of northern Iraq, at Kut, Baghdad, Mosul, and Kirkuk as well as in the swamps of lower Mesopotamia; they have scattered their goldsmith's shops and silver-jewelry stores throughout Beirut, Damascus, and Alexandria. In Iran the Ghebers (or Zoroastrians— they are survivals from the ancient Iranian religious community) now exist only as an urban or suburban community, as small traders, or above all as gardeners in the oases around towns, as at Yezd and Kerman, where they are rather oppressed, and at Teheran, Shiraz, Meshed, Isfahan, and Hamadan, where their situation is somewhat better, as well as at Baku. The Ghebers of Kerman, according to Tavernier, had a monopoly on the wool trade during the eighteenth century. They were integrated through the efforts of Shah Abbas to reorganize the cities; he installed a group of them at Isfahan, but they have since left for Yezd and Kerman, where they were converted to Islam.

Finally, the Jews throughout Islam as elsewhere are a

specifically urban minority. Wherever there are rural Jews, for example in Morocco, they have more and more difficulty in maintaining their existence. Thus the Jews of the Anti-Atlas have been radically thinned out by more or less forced conversions and by pogroms. The good relations with their neighbors achieved by the ghetto folk of Tahala in the country of the Ammeln have been studied by J. Chaumeil, but they are exceptional, so exceptional as to have made this community a sort of ghetto refuge. A certain intolerance seems to have marked rural areas, as contrasted with cities. These rural ghettos of the Anti-Atlas barely exist now because of a general movement toward the towns and retail shopkeeping in competition with the Shilha. In the last fifteen or seventeen years two ghettos have actually disappeared from the Sous. Equally unpromising is the present situation of the Jews of Debdou, a town of the Middle Atlas whose origins may be found in the arrival of Jews seeking refuge from the Spanish persecutions of 1391; the rural communities of the island of Djerba (Hara-Kebira and Hara-Sghira) are also in sore straits. More and more, rural Judaism seems doomed, and even if the creation of Israel as a state does not totally eliminate the Jews from Moslem countries it seems bound to force them toward the cities.

The occupational limitations on Jews in the cities are sometimes very strict. At Casablanca the list of specifically Jewish occupations comprises fairly humble trades such as house painters and whitewashers (but not painters of interiors, who are always Moslems), tinsmiths, glaziers, stove makers, founders and molders of copper, repairers of slippers (but not makers of new slippers), and sellers of lemonade and of eggs. In the old centers like Fez, Marrakech, and Salé the Jewish artisans are on a higher level (they are jewelers, dealing in gold and silver like the Soussi, also silk weavers and lacemakers, dealing in rare and expensive cloth); they are also more closely intermingled with the mass of other artisans.

This urban segregation has been the privilege of non-Islamic minorities, but as a result of recent changes and the extension under European influence of equal rights before the law a number of persecuted heretical sects have taken advantage of it and are now in a position to make their unorthodox energies felt on the economic level. The clearest examples are in North Africa. The Ibadites of Mount Nefusa, of Djerba and Mzab, have quitted their distant oases and their rocky crags for the great towns of the north. The Mzabites and Djerbians are retail grocers in Algiers and Tunis, respectively. In addition the Mzabites ply a number of lesser trades within the community of Algiers; they are butchers and charcoal dealers; they sell manure and sometimes make little fried cakes and pastries. The arrivals from Nefusa are butchers and distributors of bread at Tunis, and, what is more, these Berber Ibadites, unlike their Arabian countrymen, will consider emigrating. In Senegal likewise a growing urban activity engendered by colonization has encouraged the appearance within the cities of the Mourid sect, otherwise typically agrarian. Sizable groups have taken up trading at Dakar and along the railroad line as far as Agboville on the Ivory Coast. The Serignes send them out to work for the brotherhood as porters, sellers of kola in the railway stations, and artisans, for example as tailors, butchers, coal sellers, peddlers, saddlers, mattress makers, *laptots* ("boatmen or porters") on the river, and fishermen at Rufisque and Saint-Louis. Similiarly their wives do embroidery work, dressmaking, and dyeing. Still others have entered into the administration as clerks and policemen. In British East Africa the growth of the Indian trade has brought about the appearance of numerous Ismaili centers in the principal cities.

Another contemporary phenomenon that emphasizes the tendency of minorities to spread into the cities is the proliferation within Islam and along its borders of a new kind of sect, which may be called "ecumenical" or "syncretist." Often combining religious concepts of very different origins, these sects in their growth (which is sometimes world-wide) seem to be linked to the present development of international relations and of intercontinental migrations. Such is the sect of the Ahmadiya, which originated in India but has expanded to the four corners of the globe by way of Moslem Indian traders, and which possesses flourishing communities in the coastal trading cities of Black West Africa, with connections which extend as far as Europe and the United States. Another is Bahaism, a super-religion derived from Persian Babism at the end of the last century, which is today spread throughout the world, principally in large cities and especially in the United States. As for Babism itself, it hides its important influence under a cloak of respectability throughout the main cities of Iran. In this urban segregation on a world-wide scale one sees the ultimate stage in the "disincarnation" of Islamic sects as well as the complete antithesis of the traditional rural refuges.

New aspects of religious geography in the Near East. The Near East itself has been a witness to the most startling reversals. It would be improper to see there nothing but a land of quarrels dedicated to perpetual divisions. For more than a century the religious geography of this land where segregation has been the unbroken rule has been deeply disturbed. A new hierarchy of values is making itself felt in which faith no longer occupies an uncontested primacy.

The major factor is certainly the gradual abandonment of the refuges, the descent from the mountains. The return of security, dating from the opening up of the land in the second half of the nineteenth century but notably accelerated by the intervention of the powers holding mandates, has unleashed a great liberation movement, affecting most of the sects that had taken refuge in the barren and overpopulated mountains. They have moved down to a more rewarding country. Thus the Alawites (Nusairi) of Mount Ansariye have for more than a century been spreading out to the surrounding areas, to the plains of Akkar to the south and of Latakia to the west and toward El Ghab in the east. In the latter region the first localities inhabited by the Nusairi were invested in 1860. They quickly created there a number of villages, pushing the Christians and even the Sunnites back toward the plateau of Hama. This essentially peaceful advance was limited to the left bank of the Orontes, but all the eastern part of El Ghab has become the property of the Nusairi and only the fortresses of the east are left to the Sunnites. The Alawite colonization of Mamoura, from the steppes east of Homs and Hama and southwest of Aleppo as far as the bend of the Euphrates at Meskene, was accomplished by the agas of Hama. To the north the Alawites by the end of the nineteenth century had partially colonized the Cilician plain, where in the vicinity of Tarsus and Adana they number eighty thousand in Turkish territory alone.

The Ismaili have undertaken a similar migration, starting from their fortresses atop the Alawite range. Since the middle of the nineteenth century, when it was encouraged by the Emir Ismail, an important colony has existed in the region of Selemiya, to the east of Hama and at the edge of the Syrian desert. This was formerly the captial of the sect and typical of the desert type of refuge. It had been gradually abandoned after the tenth century, while the country returned to nomadism. At first Ismaili emigration was seasonal; later it became more stable. In addition to the ideal of resurrecting their ancient religious center, the Ismaili had the precious economic stimulus of fertile lands to reclaim, and their enterprise worked marvels. Today from 25,000 to 35,000 of them live around Selemiya, as against fewer than 10,000 in their mountain retreat, and their community is in the full flux of prosperity. It has often been noted that the character of this sect has changed remarkably and that the economic and social changes which are at work in the whole Near East have operated here with unusual rapidity. Among the Christian Maronites of the Lebanese mountains the process is infinitely slower. It is only in

"Little Lebanon," where change has been able to work more freely, that the sectarians have ventured to descend in some numbers toward the seashore and the cities (and even here they have not yet become very numerous in the biggest cities). In the vicinity of Saida to the south and Tripoli to the north they hold faithfully to the ancient geographical divisions of the population. These Christians, who from ancient times have been oriented to the West, take more freely to overseas emigration than to descent into the plains; more than a third of the whole community has passed across the Lebanese border.

Finally, the Tahtadjis of the Taurus range exhibit the same tendency, though somewhat modified by the particular conditions of their way of life. Their foothold in Anatolian cities is of long standing, dating back at least to the sixteenth century, and within the cities they constituted thriving communities of carpenters. But until the nineteenth century they lived in the mountains whenever they lived in the country. Since the second half of the nineteenth century they have begun spreading out on the lower Aegean and Mediterranean plains around the circumference of the high Anatolian plateau; this movement cannot be specifically distinguished from that which has generally affected the seminomads of Asia Minor. The Tahtadjis first settled primarily in wooded sections, either on the border or at the approaches to great wooded ranges (on the plain of Finike and the outskirts of Günnük near the great woodworking center of Fethiye, which developed at this period in lower Lycia). Since the passage of a law in 1937 restricting woodcutting and thus eliminating their traditional occupation their dispersion has grown much wider and more various. Even their way of life has often been modified. Those who live at Naldoken near Izmir (Smyrna) have become masons and furnish limestone to the entire district. Other movements of the same nature have not been altogether spontaneous. The Assyro-Nestorians, who ever since the Mongolian invasions had been refugees in the mountainous parts of Kurdistan, were largely driven out by the war of 1914–1918 and by the aftermath of the Kurdish revolt of 1925. A tiny minority still subsists in the Hakari Mountains or in the upland plains around Lake Urmia, but the remainder have moved for the most part into upper Syrian Jezire, that great area of contemporary colonization within the Fertile Crescent.

Another basic characteristic of modern development, one which complements previous trends though it is basically unconnected with them, is a general tendency for minorities to be absorbed and to disappear. The little isolated rural minorities have been subjected to more and more vigorous processes of assimilation, and residual elements have gone far toward losing their individuality entirely. This has happened, for example, to the Yazidis of Syria (on Mount Siman), who continue to exist only by means of constant reinforcements brought in to fill the gaps caused by a process of conversion to Islam which has been going on for a long time. It has happened, too, to the Druse community of Israel (inhabiting Mount Carmel and Upper Galilee), which in 1949 constituted no more than 49 per cent of the population of its seventeen villages (as against 58 per cent in 1931), and this in spite of an unquestioned natural increase in absolute numbers. Many of these little rural groups, finding their existence threatened, moved toward urban centers (the Ismaili of the mountains for example), in conformity with the general modern process of urbanization described above.

Thus these two factors join to weaken the old lines of differentiation. By expansion or by dispersion religious communities lose the marked individuality they once had. A regrouping of the population is under way by virtue of economic conditions that affect in identical ways groups which are essentially quite different. Another sort of minority is far from giving way, the minority which is founded on language and culture. Ethnic antagonisms are more lively than ever. As early as 1934 J. Weulersse noted shrewdly that the danger to the state of Iraq came not from the Shiites, though they were a numerical majority in this land of a Sunnite dynasty, but from the Kurds, whose religion was the same as that of the governors. In the grouping of peoples nationality has tended to replace religion. National minorities appear to be irreducible, whereas religious minorities either disappear entirely or else transform themselves into national minorities. Religious geography within Islam is being smothered, is losing its clarity; one can foresee its effacement.

CHAPTER III

Geographical Factors in the Expansion of Islam

HAVING studied in the previous chapters the imprint that Islam has left on manners of life and modes of tilling the soil, as well as its self-divisions, we may now undertake to look at the other side of the coin. To what extent is Islam itself the expression of a specific geographical environment? In other words, is the map of Islam determined, and, if so, in what degree by geographical and natural circumstances? At the outset one can scarcely fail to be struck by the remarkable coincidence between the area dominated by Islam and desert areas, or, at the very least, areas with a pronounced dry season. When Islamic lands do not have an absolute deficiency in rainfall, they at least experience a notable seasonal lack of it. If we except Bengal and Indonesia as outskirts, there seems to be an almost absolute identity between the limits of Islam and those of the arid and semiarid regions of the ancient

world.[1] This identity is even more marked if we recall
that the whole Mediterranean area was formerly unified
under the aegis of Islam, before the period of withdrawal
that ended by almost completely eliminating the Moslems
from the northern coast of that sea. At any rate the heart
of Islam remains that desert zone which, slanting across
the globe from the Atlantic Ocean to Central Asia, includes the whole of the ancient world between, on the
one side, the humid zones of intertropical Africa and
monsoon-moistened Asia and, on the other side, the wet
and temperate climate of Europe. Is this a matter, as someone has said recently, of a "geographical accident," [2] or
does it reflect an intimate correspondence between this
type of environment on the one hand and the demands
and capabilities of the Moslem religion on the other hand?

Ways in which Islam expanded and types of frontiers.
Islam knows two basic ways of expanding, one by the
holy war, the jihad, the other by peaceful means, such as
are now being given free play in Black Africa under
French and British authority. In fact the two methods are
not sharply differentiated, for Islamic toleration with regard to the "religions of the book" often allows them to
survive after Moslem conquest; and even conquest, except
when attended by forced conversions, creates only conditions which are particularly favorable to the developing process of conversion to Islam but none which are

[1] See, for example, the aridity index map of De Martonne,
Annales de géographie, 1942.
[2] Fernau, *Flackernder Halbmond* (Zurich, 1953), tr. into
French under the title *Le réveil du monde musulman* (Paris,
1956).

fundamentally different from those in countries where Islam does not hold political power. The development of powerful Moslem political organizations has often lagged far behind the general extension of Islamic religion through occupied countries (i.e., the Ottoman Empire and the Mongol Empire of India). Arabization has evidently hastened the process of conversion, but not even Arabization has been decisive (as in the Near East) or even necessary (as in Berber North Africa and Iran) for the complete triumph of Islam.

The limit of lands subjected to Islamic sway (*dar al-Islam*), which was achieved by holy war, corresponds to an equilibrium of political forces. It simply expresses the results of historical events. The forces of nature scarcely influence it at all except as the earth's surface (i.e., mountain ranges) lends itself to defense. The other essential factor has to do with political and social order and with the more or less determined cohesion of the non-Islamic societies and states in conflict with the Moslem world along its periphery. The limits imposed by these forces are fragile and fluctuating. Their precariousness is evidenced by the spectacular setbacks which Islam sometimes suffers when a superficial conversion to Islam, which had accompanied the establishment of Moslem power, disappears with it. Yet these limitations have a real influence on the extent of the Moslem religion whenever the rule of Islam is sufficiently stable. There is actually no real rule to govern the importance of forced conversions, which have often been of capital significance.

At present we can observe only the peaceful expansion

of Islam. The ways in which Islam was spread to the accompaniment of force and violence can only be analyzed through historical research, and they remain largely mysterious to us. Only the methods of expansion currently in use allow us to determine with some exactness the principal elements in Islam's favor and the chief obstacles to be overcome in its continued growth. Thus the limits achieved by peaceful means are more revealing than those achieved by force. This peaceful expansion takes place essentially through city people and commercial centers. The expansion of Islam seems therefore to be linked to means of communication; the religion spreads along trade routes and in coastal areas but is hindered by all natural obstacles to social life (mountain ranges and densely forested areas) as well as by the simple inertia of the rural population. The peaceful limits of Islam are, as it were, the limits of a set of tentacles. The Moslem religion may be thought of as a sort of gigantic octopus, the arms of which reach far down the main roads and project far in front of the animal's actual body. Geographical influences are of the utmost importance here, but only insofar as historical and economic conditions give an advantage to one route or another at one moment of history or another. The obstacles set up by society naturally continue in full force, since everything which reinforces the traditional society, the traditional mentality, is opposed to the development of a new religion.

In the past, so far as one can tell, the different processes of expansion were nearly always combined and in different proportions. The victory of Islam brought about the immediate appearance of an urban Moslem class of administrators and traders, who embarked at once on a program of proselytizing, reinforcing the appeal of their religious ideas by the use of political suasion and emphasis on the considerable advantages accompanying conversion. On the other hand, expansion along trade routes often brought about the conversion to Islam of small princely courts, where the purity of religion was apt to be spotted, notably by mixed marriages but also in petty local wars. The mixture of various elements appears in most cases to have been very delicately proportioned; the frontiers of Islam were complexly structured; and a detailed analysis of each particular region is therefore called for.

The African frontiers of Islam. In Black Africa, Islam has used its two different methods of expansion one after the other. Although it was warlike until the coming of white colonizers, the Moslem advance has become peaceful since the Europeans arrived and has in general gone considerably faster since that date, turning the flank of obstacles which it could never take by assault. These new conditions, however, date back no more than a half or at most three-quarters of a century. The frontier of Islam still remains as it was determined in its general outline by the equilibrium of political and social forces that existed before white colonization. But in its details the line of the frontier has been deeply modified and broken into on every side.

A particularly clear example of the influence of geographical factors is supplied by the frontier of Islam in Ethiopia. A settled Christian civilization has maintained itself there in the uplands of Tigre and Shoa, surrounded

on every side except the southwest by Islamic populations.
A little to the east, in Eritrea, the dividing line between
Christianity and Islam is almost identical with the dividing line between settled and nomadic populations (in
Eritrea only the Mansa, the Bait Juk, and the Bilen of the
region northwest of Massawa have been partially converted to Islam, even though they are settled peoples).
Should we then attribute the persistence of Christianity
in Ethiopia solely to the defensive advantages of the
Ethiopian mountain ranges, as Toynbee does? By itself,
this geographical factor is not always decisive. In the sixteenth century the conquest of the highlands by Imam
Ahmed left its traces in the form of Islamic agricultural
colonies in the very center of the Christian zone (this is
the origin of a part of the Jabarti, who are Moslems in the
Christian regions of Ethiopia). Shortly afterward the
Galla tribes regained the whole eastern and southeastern
part of the upper plateau, where they were subsequently
converted to Islam. In fact, we must attribute part of
Christianity's exceptional resistance here to the weakness
of the attack. For in Ethiopia, Islam did not follow on the
heels of Arabization. It was introduced by nomad Hamitic tribes that remained culturally autonomous. They
acquired their Islamic convictions in the little trading establishments on the coast of eastern Africa by the familiar
process of meeting with merchants and forming matri-
monial alliances with princely families, but without any
initial violent impact. The process of Arabization was
much weaker here than, for example, in Nilotic Sudan.

Why such a difference? Is it, as Trimingham supposes,
a consequence of the fact that the Dongola plains had

few attractions, even for nomadic Arabs? Actually it is more a question of the geographical situation of Ethiopia in relation to the great currents of nomadic Arabian expansion, which are traditionally directed from south to north, toward the Fertile Crescent. As it left Arabia, Islam expanded according to the natural path of pastoral migrations. Ethiopia, on the very edge of this current, was faced only by the Yemenites, sedentary and unaggressive. The attack by Sudan came much later, and scarcely became serious before the nineteenth century.

For this reason too the expansion of Islam at the expense of the Christian kingdoms of Maqurra and Alwa, the first of which was overrun in the fourteenth and the second at the beginning of the sixteenth century, was both late and slow, taking place long after Islam had spread through western Africa. In fact there was never even a question of violent conquest. Infiltration was accomplished by a process of intermixture, by Moslem intermarriage with the nomad societies, leading gradually to the disintegration of the traditional social structure. The drive of the nomad tribes to the south has always been weak, motivated as much, and perhaps more, by the desire to escape from the Mamelukes as by the desire for new pastures. Thus the devotion of central Sudan to Islam has always been lukewarm in the past. To the east of the Nile the Moslem religion has had little success in its dealings with the seminomads who raise large cattle. West of the river the Nubas used to be limited to hill country, which they cultivated by means of terraces (to the south of El Obeid in the Kordofan), and from which they fought off the warlike advances of slave traders. The modern era of

peace has brought about some advances for Islam, since
the Nubas have come down from their hills and gone to
work in the plains amid a purely Islamic environment.
But the Nilotics (Shilluk, Nuer) have maintained their
tribal organization intact, and Islam has been unable to
gain a foothold.

In Black West Africa, on the other hand, the expansion of Islam occurred much earlier and was essentially
warlike in character. It took place along two basic lines.
In the west Islam depended on the Hamitic and Fulah
peoples of Berber origin; and since the fall of the Empire
of Ghana (1240) they have been the cornerstones of great
political edifices, which usually accomplished little in the
way of converting their domains to Islam. Religious con-
viction among those peoples remained superficial, all the
more so because this part of Islam had been cut off from
Mecca ever since the Middle Ages, was weakened by
belief in *baraka,* or the "supernatural power of certain
persons and objects," and the cult of saints, and so de-
generated easily into magic practices which made it acceptable to the animists but left it little in common with
Islam proper. Reformed by the Fulah in the eighteenth
century, it was carried forward by these pastoral folk
from Fouta Djallon, an area which was itself colonized
in the seventeenth century. The Toucouleur Empire and
the warring states at the end of the nineteenth century
(Samory), though their downfall was sometimes accompanied by the surrender of an Islamic faith too rapidly
acquired, generally brought about a much more intense
phase of Islamic feeling. The other current, which passed
by way of the Chad and was typically Negro-Arab, drew

on the currents of a much more intense spiritual life and, though more limited in its expansion, doubtless worked at greater depth. These two lines of expansion correspond to the two great paths across the Sahara Desert, that of the Chad and that of the western, Moorish Sahara, and to the injection of Nordic cultural elements, which were early transferred to the pastoral populations.

The blocks of resistance to these currents of Islamic migration have been stable political constructions on the part of the animist peoples rather than natural obstacles. (In East Africa the mountain ranges and the grassy upland plateaus destined for pastures have often even constituted solid points of support for the advance of Islam.) These animist kingdoms were essentially the Bambara and Mossi Empires. The first absorbed the impact of the southern Islamic empires in the western basin of the Niger, but its disappearance as an independent political unit left the Bambara country wide open to the influence of Islam. The Mossi Empire, on the other hand, has continued till the present day to constitute an almost impenetrable obstacle. E. F. Gautier has discussed the causes of this resistance. It is a country with old traditions, with a solid royal authority, and a regular government, safe from internal revolutions. The land of the Mossi is good for raising millet, crops are abundant, and horses can be bred in quantity (there is a horse for every 25 inhabitants as against a horse for every 160 inhabitants in nearby nations). Finally, it is a land rich in laterite, where there exist the rudiments of an iron industry. All this might be the result of a technical and social superiority linked to mysterious trans-Saharan influences (perhaps Carthaginian?).

The latter ideas have been soundly criticized by Y. Urvoy,[3] who denies that the Mossi land has any special "affinity" resulting in densities of population and plantation but sees in its present character simply a historical event, corresponding to a temporary phase, a state of affairs which once existed farther to the west until the end of the Bambara Empire, quite out of range of these pretended influences. But whether the reasons for it are sought in remote cultural influences or in a simple historical accident, the fact of Mossi resistance has had the greatest consequences in barring Islam from the road to the lower Ivory Coast.

Another element of resistance, this time natural in character, has been the great forest of central Africa. Islam has almost never been able to penetrate this great forest, and in the history of the Islamic frontier there are innumerable examples when the religion of the open plain came to a dead halt before thickly forested areas, allowing them to remain animist (for example, the now-devastated forest of Thor Diander in Senegal, certain Serer districts of Sine Saloum, and the wooded areas inhabited by the Diulas in Casamance). Is it a question here, as Governor de Coppet has said, of an affinity which wooded regions have for polymorphism, for divine forces scattered everywhere through the shadows, the darkness, and the silence and easily available to the conjuring of sorcerers, as against the single God of the open plains? In fact the forest has always acted against Islam, simply as an obstacle to the penetration of shepherds (on the biological level the wide diffusion of trypanosomes is par-

[3] *Petit atlas ethno-démographique du Soudan* (Paris, 1940).

ticularly effective), but also as an obstacle to traders, who have nonetheless founded prosperous Islamic colonies in the main forested areas, along the great arteries of circulation, and in the clearings.

The fact is that since the colonial pacification the main job of propagating the Moslem religion has been undertaken by merchants and traders, Mande-Diulas to the west, Hausas to the east. In their wake the "saints" and schoolmasters are installed, and these formal propagandists profit by the prestige of their commercial predecessors; in a sense they simply cause the dough to rise which had previously been mixed. It would be useless to list the innumerable colonies that Islam has thus scattered through the zone of deep forests, essentially in the cities and along the coasts, where the Moslems coming from the north often discover Moslems of other origins. For example, in Lower Dahomey the origins of Islam must be sought in certain black Moslem slaves from South America, who returned to Africa after their liberation and settled at Petit-Popo and Lagos, where they established curious mixed sects, both Christian and Moslem at once (one of them at Porto-Novo worships "Sidi Mohammed, *defender of the faith*"). This commercial penetration is backed up by a more and more active program of proselytizing, which overrides all efforts at counterpropaganda by the animist groups, who in any case are gradually being menaced with disintegration as a result of contemporary economic conditions. Thus the Mossi, when they leave their country to work on the cacao plantations of the Gold Coast, fall easy prey to the converters as soon as they leave their traditional social milieu. Military service is equal to migrations in search of work as an effective instrument in converting men to Islam.

In central, eastern, and southeastern Africa Moslem expansion is continuing energetically in an area that has practically never been touched by Islamic warriors, if one excepts a few forced conversions accomplished on the shores of eastern Africa by slave merchants. In South Africa, Islam is represented mainly by Indian traders. In eastern Africa also it has followed the trade routes, notably those leading out of Zanzibar. It has reached as far as the Belgian Congo, where strong groups of Islamic converts are found, as for example at Usumbura (they are Swahili traders who include a large proportion of Ismaili) and as far as Stanleyville and Leopoldville, where the Islamic movement encounters certain sympathetic "Senegalese" traders coming from eastern Africa. Just recently Islam has started to depart from its traditional limits and extend its influence into the countryside. It is gaining a foothold in the brush and in the newly formed mining towns, profiting, as in French West Africa, from the breakup of the old tribal patterns. In eastern Africa it has reached into the always-receptive pastoral peoples, like the Massai, where the process of conversion has recently begun. We have already noted a certain classification by altitude in commenting on the importance of the healthy climate found in the upland areas of eastern Africa for the success of this religion of an arid land. Spreading out below the levels of European colonization, where the settlers occupy the very highest plateaus, the Moslem still remains higher than his fellow natives, who live in the lower and less healthy regions.

The European and Central Asiatic frontier. At present Islam is entrenched on the southern and eastern coasts of the Mediterranean, but the shores of Europe seem likely to be, henceforth, beyond its reach. In the western Mediterranean it is evidently the dividing line of the sea itself, and it is the greater density of population in Turkish Anatolia as compared with the density of population in the Balkans, which have limited its withdrawal before the technical and military superiority of Europeans. But if the Mediterranean frontier of Islam is thus largely "strategic" today, what was its nature at the time of the farthest Islamic advance? E. F. Gautier has observed that the farthest advance of Islam in the western Mediterranean coincided almost exactly with the limits of the Carthaginian occupation; they recovered the western part of Sicily (the valley of Mazara and the city of Palermo, while the valley Demone, a mountainous area to the north and east, remained Christian and free with the exception of Messina; and they took the valley of Noto, while the province of Syracuse remained Christian, though it paid tribute to Islam). In Spain, Islam overran the central part of the peninsula, where its most stable limits were, in large measure, those imposed by nature on the growth of the olive tree. Here we have an "oriental domain," "a line of cleavage, beyond which the Arabian empire did not find in the human subconscious, in the powerful kingdom of dead history, any Punic memories." [4] In fact this frontier also marks the weariness of Islamic conquerors in the face of natural obstacles like the mountain ranges of east-

[4] Gautier, *Mœurs et coutumes des Musulmans* (Paris, 1931), p. 192.

ern and northeastern Sicily (which are also farther from Africa) or like the high plateus of the Spanish Meseta, where Islamic colonization was never accomplished except by Berbers. The Arabs never got beyond the low plains of the south and had to use Berber intermediaries· to occupy the highlands, where the climate repelled them so effectively that not even the North African mountaineers could adjust to life in the Iberian Peninsula.

In the Balkans natural factors also had great influence. The maps of Islamic populations there at different stages show that these people were strictly localized by the great trade routes and that they were limited to the plains, whereas the Christian populations occupied the mountain ranges. These mountain ranges, heavily wooded with oak trees and supporting a fine population of pigs (for example, the Serbian range of Choumada), quite naturally became refuges for the Christian populations. A notable exception is that of the Bosnian Moslems, recruited for the most part from among mountaineers (the most thoroughly Islamized areas of the Balkans were Krajina in the northwest, which was a bastion of Islam and a center for warfare, and the region of Sarajevo, which was a cultural and economic center). Conversion was certainly made easier by the presence among these Christians of the Bogomil heresy, which forbade the eating of all meat and thus throughout the region limited the raising of pork. On the other hand, the forced conversion of the Pomaks of Rhodope during the seventeenth century seems to have been nothing whatever but a political accident. In the Caucasus the resistance that centered in the mountains was of the same order. Islamization took place at the two ends of the mountain range (more slowly in the west among the Circassians under Turkish influence) and steered clear of the Georgian Christians in the center. From Spain to the Caucasus the northern frontier of Islam was ever a battle front, and the part played by natural obstacles seems to have been determining.

It was not quite the same in Central Asia. Certain very remote influences are linked here to phases of an essentially warlike expansion. (The Moslems of Yunnan, for example, seem to derive from the settling down of a group of Tartar soldiers who had served Kubla Khan after the Mongols destroyed the empire of Nan-Chao in 1227.) But on the whole Islam never unleashed the holy war in Central Asia; the religion did not change the general direction of Turkish expansion, which was toward the west. In addition the arrival of Islam among the Turks was relatively slow and late. During the first eras of Islamic domination over Central Asia (the seventh and eighth centuries) there even occurred several important victories for Manichaeism and Christianity under the new regime. For a long time the frontier of Islam remained the limits of the settled Persians. When the prestige of these settled peoples as craftsmen and traders had brought the nomads across the Oxus to a peaceful acceptance of Islam, the Turks suddenly appointed themselves zealous apostles of the religion. (Cf. the text of Mahmud al-Kashgari, putting in the mouth of God the famous phrase: "I have an army of people whom I have called Turks, and whom I have placed in the Orient. When a people rouses my wrath, I give them power in order to subdue them.") The expansion of Islam along the trade routes of Central Asia north as well as south of the desert of Takla-Makan was accomplished primarily by traders and clerks in the service of the Qara-Qitay. The Ouigours gave to all Moslems the name of Tchermaq, a name used in southern Russia to describe itinerant peddlers who drove about in wagons. About the time of Marco Polo, Islam reached as far as Lob Nor, which still belonged to the infidels in the days of Mahmud al-Kashgari (1073). At the same time, on the route running north of the Tarim Basin, it scarcely reached beyond Kuldja. Islamic military undertakings were always very limited. This explains why the diffusion of Islam took place solely along the trade routes of Turkestan, whence it penetrated to China (a very small section of the Chinese Moslems derives from a settlement made by sea at Canton). On its way eastward Islam entirely neglected easy conquests on the Mongol steppes or in the wooded regions to the north, because these were marginal to the main trade lines. The Islamization of the Golden Horde was simply a historical accident. Passing between Buddhist Mongolia and Tibet, the Moslem advance to Turkestan (which is linked in part to the Turkish peoples) expresses above all the existence of the transcontinental commercial route to China, along the linked oases of the Tarim Basin.

The appendages of Southeast Asia. In India the expansion of Islam was essentially the work of a conquering minority. In northwestern India its frontier remained identical with the end of the arid zone, and the map showing strong concentrations of Islamic believers clearly coincides there with the map showing small amounts of rainfall. Resistance by rural communities in the plain of the Ganges and northwest of the Deccan has impeded its progress. But interpenetration is very advanced, and the details are complex. In the central provinces Moslem density is clearly related to the time and density of settlement of the land by Rajputs, warriors and fanatical adversaries of Islam; there are fewer Moslems wherever there are more Rajputs and wherever their establishment is of ancient date. In the rest of India, Islam, in spite of periods of persecution (before the period of Mongol tolerance and again after Aurangzeb) could develop only weak minorities. A notable exception is found in eastern Bengal, where low-caste Hindus were converted en masse, culminating in a kind of Islamic extremism that made them easy prey for movements like Wahhabism. The Moslem religion is strictly limited to the plain and stops short at the first outworks of Assam. In southern India and Ceylon, on the other hand, Islamic influence has been notable chiefly along the seacoasts and at the terminals of commercial and maritime routes. It has been marked by the formation of groups of intermarried Arabs and natives (the "Moors" of Ceylon). Thus the Indian frontier combines three elements, a battleground linked with climatic influences in the northwest, a secondary front where social circumstances determine in Bengal, and trading colonies in the peninsula and along the southern coast line.

Indonesia is a typical example of Islam's expansion along commercial and maritime trade routes. Maritime relations with India, facilitated by the alternation of the monsoons, were the essential vehicle. The classic theory of Snouck-Hurgronje on the Islamization of Java presumes that before any contact with Arabia the Javanese were influenced by Moslem merchants from India, not as conquerors but as the founders of markets and the converters of native women. Thus at the beginning the process of conversion would have been essentially peaceful, and war against the unbelievers in the interior began only after the seacoast cities were converted. This theory has been corrected in some of its major tenets by Schrieke, who insisted on the role of princely marriages in the Indonesian courts, in addition to the action of the merchants, and on the psychological appeal of Islam to the "proud" Javanese as an alternative to Hinduism. The theory has been almost contradicted by Van Leur and later by Berg. According to Berg, the merchant would not have the prestige, the necessary social superiority, to propagate Islam. This is accomplished exclusively by the conversion of princes, hastened or retarded by the caprices of the individual, and linked to favorable factors, such as the expansion of Islam in India, with a resultant decline in Brahmanism, the animosity between coastal princes and the kings of the interior, or the common front with the Moslems against the Portuguese, hereditary enemies of Islam. Certain spectacular conversions were purely tactical. Whatever the exact methods by which this movement advanced and whatever its particular instruments, Islam was nonetheless carried by merchants and along commercial routes even if the conversion of princes was linked to political contingencies.

In the minutiae Islamic penetration is linked to means of social communication. Backward and isolated groups in the interior of the islands held out against it (for example, the Batak country around Lake Toba on Sumatra, whereas the area south of the Batak country, around the transverse depression that links it to the Menangkabau country, has been strongly influenced by Islam and was even touched in the nineteenth century by Wahhabism; likewise the Dayak country in the interior of Borneo and the Torodja country in the interior of Celebes). There have also been centers of resistance in the outlying districts (the Badoujesen group of Java in the south where the Bantam are found or the Minahassan in the north of Celebes). There are also island refuges, like Bali, just east of Java, the dense population of which is explained by the concentration of Hindus fleeing Islam, and there are frontier "vacuums," as the extreme eastern part of Java, which lies between the Moslems of Java and the Hindus of Bali, or the southern part of the Philippine Archipelago, which is a land of struggle between the Moors of Mindanao and the Christians of the north. In the Moluccas the influence of Islam is limited to traditional commercial and political centers (Jolo in the Sulu Archipelago). In French Indochina the influence of Islam is limited to the southeastern frontier, among the coastal Chams, who are remnants of the oldest political organization in the country and who were probably influenced by commercial centers in their vicinity. There are also some immigrant Malays who profess Islam. The rest of the country lay outside the main trade routes and was not touched by the Moslem invasions on the continent.

This very superficial conversion of Indonesia to Islam, for a long time limited to the rather casual conversion of princes, has achieved nothing but a cultural symbiosis, within which the place of Islam is not well defined. The dense agrarian societies of these lands have shown themselves relatively resistant to Islam. Only the permanence and continuity of its cultural relations have been able to secure it even nominal success.

Madagascar was for Islam an abortive Indonesia. The propagating action of the original elements, whether traders from Zanzibar or the Cornoro Islands, or even Arabians driven by the monsoon from the northeast, was not sufficiently strong or sustained, since communications were infrequent and irregular. A certain number of tribes have accepted Islam, but the Malagasy Moslems, both those of the northwest coast and those southeast of the island, are often Moslems in name only. G. Ferrand has seen the basic reason for this setback as the "state of nature" of the Malagasy, whom he thinks unconvertible because too barbarous. More simply, and as the same author has elsewhere remarked, the road that led to Madagascar was too weak and narrow to bring powerful cultural influences. No syncretic cultural system, such as was established in the Malay States, could ever get started, although the human materials at its disposal seemed at the beginning to have certain affinities with those of Indonesia.

Conclusion: The limits of Islam. We are now ready to provide at least a partial answer to the question posed at the beginning of this chapter. Why has Islam never been able, with rare exceptions, to encroach seriously on any of the zones of dense rural population which surround the arid zone on the northwest, the south, and the southeast? What is the major obstacle that has opposed its further progress? This review of the different regional circumstances provides an idea of the extreme complexity characterizing Islamic frontiers. But the salient outlines are easy to distinguish.

Let us eliminate, first of all, the minor factors. In certain peasant communities prohibition of particular foods has been sufficient to hold back its progress. In the oak-forested Balkan mountains or in the area of Chinese civilization the ban on pork has slowed down conversions. The same thing can hardly be said of the ban on wine in Mediterranean areas, and we have seen what flexibility Islam can display, within its borders, in regard to these bans, what adjustments can be made. It is impossible to see here anything but a secondary factor, which may have rendered the progress of the Moslem religion more difficult but could not possibly bear major responsibility for its defeats. It is the same with the morphological factors and with the influence of the vegetable kingdom. Elevations and depressions of the land surface seem to influence only frontier details, not its general course, and the direction of their influence is often contradictory. As for the great forests, they do constitute a serious obstacle in Black Africa to the expansion of Islam. But the human will can conquer them. The forests offer rewards to apostles. If Islam has so far scarcely penetrated the forest, the reason is that so far it has hardly tried.

A more general theory has been put forward by J. Célerier. According to this theory, Islam, a religion of fatalism and resignation, is unsuited to the cool climate of the temperate zone, which is particularly favorable to human effort. It is limited to the regions between the tropics, where the climate is oppressive, and its present expansion to the southward is caused by its material and moral affinities with the populations which it finds there. The equatorial zone is thus destined to offer it a particularly favorable area for future expansion. This is the rough outline of a theory of climatic determinism rather different in its ideas from a previous theory conceived by E. Huntington,[5] who contrasted the dynamic activity of men in countries having cyclonic weather and rapid changes of pressure with the passivity which prevails in countries having anticyclonic weather systems. Célerier's theory is essentially the same sort of interpretation of human evolution. Yet Islam has prevailed over a large part of the Mediterranean zone, that traditional home of dynamic thought and effective action, where the languid influence of the tropical summer is largely countered by the agitations of winter. And the present Mediterranean frontier of Islam is fixed so that it coincides least with the profound inclinations of the population and most with the outcome of simple historical events.

Must we admit, then, that Islam displays a basic incapacity to deal with densely populated rural areas, that it is so remote from the peasant mind, that its attitude toward agrarian life is so categorically hostile, that it simply cannot accommodate itself to intensive cultivation of the soil? Such a view seems excessive. The exceptions of Southeast Asia prove that, though Islam is not deep-rooted there, it is not incompatible with veritable human anthills that are perfectly stable. Within the arid and semi-arid zone itself Islam is the religion of millions of peasants,

[5] *Civilization and Climate* (New Haven, 1924).

fellahs of the Nile Delta or the Saharan oases, as well as tree growers of the Mediterranean mountain sides, all as deeply rooted in the soil as it is possible to be. A purely psychological explanation of Islam's boundaries is evidently inadequate.

Although the relation is clear, the mechanism is more complex than our theories have yet made clear. If Islam is not incompatible with peasant life, it is certainly very acceptable to the nomads, who are deeply impressed with the simplicity of this theism and the primacy of faith. It is significant that nowhere (with a partial and startling exception in Jordan) have Christian nomads been able to subsist, although peasant Christianity has often outlasted its oppressors. Spreading early through the nomads of Arabia, Islam found in the shepherds of the arid zone a particularly fertile field for the new gospel. Although they were only mediocre practitioners of the new faith, these nomads made zealous apostles. The frontiers of Islam seem to coincide very generally with those of pastoral nomadism, or at least with regions that the nomads could influence politically. It is apparent that although these forces have been able to overflow the arid or semi-arid zone in a series of quick, impressive triumphs they have not been able to make a serious, permanent impact on lands that nature destined for permanent occupation or that lie far beyond the natural limits of nomadism. The contrast between the Islamic and Christian shores of the Mediterranean shows perfectly this difference between a shore completely controlled by nomads, who find their natural home in the neighboring deserts, and a shore unified into a solid peasant civilization, against which invasions simply peter out. The conversions to Islam of Anatolia (it is entirely in the rainy, temperate zone but in its center has almost the character of an open plain and has been swept by important waves of nomadic migration) and of the Maghreb were the "terminal" successes of Islam. It has never been really domesticated on the Balkan Peninsula. In the lowlands between the tropics its expansion was linked principally to that of pastoral peoples coming from the north, until it was taken up by the traders.

Another element governing its success is to be sought in the conditions of rural life prevailing in these arid and semiarid zones. By its very nature the country there is an oasis, dependent on a nearby urban nucleus, and more or less separated from other centers of rural activity by a no-man's-land which is overrun by Arabs. The town exerts a more persistent and forceful influence on the country there than it does in the temperate zone; the countryside is more subordinate to the city; the psychological atmosphere of the townsman spreads more widely through an agrarian circle which, despite its density, is often no more than a farming and truck-gardening suburb. It is clearly in this zone of nuclear populations that Islam, an urban religion from the beginning, found conditions most favorable to its progress in a rural society.

Finally, this arid zone is marked by solidly organized commercial relations in the fixed system of caravan commerce. The mark Islam made on the commercial classes explains its vast diffusion of ideas and things along those channels that have always directed its progress and rendered its cultural impact particularly strong. Outside the arid zone its successes in Southeast Asia can only be explained as the effect of the particularly long and deep exposure of this area to these commercial apostles. The role of the sea route to the Indes, with regular trade relations favored by the monsoons, has been crucial in the diffusion of Islam. From the European Mediterranean to Indonesian waters Islam has been a religion of seamen. As for the Far East, China and Japan have been protected from Islam as much by their maritime isolation as by the resistance to infiltration of their rural populations. Islam has thus spread along the cross routes (J. Despois): the land route from the southwest to the northeast over the dry zone of the ancient world, where its dissemination has been accomplished by nomads, and the sea route from the northwest to the southeast, the "route of the Indies," where it has been propagated by seamen.

Thus the relation of cause and effect between the natural environment of Islam and the area of its domain seems unquestionable. But the operation of physical factors is subtle, and their influence is indirect. In the arid zone Moslem methods of expansion could operate freely, and that is why this area was so easily conquered. The dense and coherent rural societies of Europe and monsoon Asia put up a ferocious resistance against the nomads, and that is why Islam could not overcome them. As for the fundamental antipathy of Islam for the land, it is undeniable, but its effects would never have been decisive in isolation.

CHAPTER IV

Conclusion

A RELIGION of town dwellers and merchants, propagated by nomads, scornful of the land and those who work it, markedly separate from the soil and as unfavorable to the formation of national organisms as to that of regional alliances, Islam is, in its attitude toward material things, the living expression of the geographical and social milieu found in the caravan cities where it arose. On the other hand, it has had a strong influence on the lands that it has controlled and the modes of life that it has dominated. Islam, a powerful spiritual motivating force, is revealed as both an unusual geographic agency and a privileged instrument of expansion and influence —and the latter much more than other great monotheistic religions. Behind an apparent suppleness of interpretation operates the strong pressure of custom. Islam, which does not divide religion from society, is essentially conformist. It is a true *Weltanschauung* which covers all human activity. By what seems like a paradox, this "urban" religion has through its strictly theocratic organization fettered the harmonious development of cities, at the same time that the peasant life has remained dull, oppressed, and without initiative. Likewise the long-standing dominance of nomad groups has impeded the development of those local interconnections that form the complex groundwork of regional unities and the basis of every effort at rational exploitation of different environments.

The geographical domain of Islam, if one excepts the foreign adjuncts of Southeast Asia, appears singularly suited to its needs. It is a region where riches come not from the country, the flat land, but from the town, or oasis settlement, where Islam has long been able to pursue its destiny as an intermediary, or an intercontinental bridge. Aside from occasional accidents of conquest or nomadic raids, the limits of Islam have never been able to spread across a continental land mass beyond the arid or semiarid zone, outside the Mediterranean region or the tropical swamplands. One may perhaps find in this inmost preference certain causes of the hardened arteries of Islam. If it is true that great historical conquests have been achieved only by solid rural civilizations, then Islam can only have been destined for ephemeral achievements. The isolation of settlements in this region has worked strongly against any effort at social revival ever since the age when the great intercontinental trade routes bypassed Islam in favor of ocean travel. Since then the cities scattered widely across deserts and steppes have been unable to find in their immediate environment the basis of a new prosperity.

As J. Célerier has well noted, the division of Islam into isolated units is incompatible with the fundamental need for unity in the Islamic world. The geographical idea of a zone works against a unified political structure. Open zonal space has favored indefinite expansion in the same direction—great circular impulses scarcely touched by drives toward the north and predatory imperialisms quick to spring up and unstable once they have appeared. These tendencies have taken place at the expense of slow national growths linked to the development of several complementary economies. Arising as it does from a precisely defined environment and mentality, Islam found in these very influences the seeds of its rapid triumphs, but also of its failures, its compulsions, its limitations.

Bibliography*

Cet ouvrage, par sa nature même, est tributaire, souvent pour des détails infimes, d'une foule d'ouvrages généraux sur l'Islam, de sources de renseignements d'ensemble (telle l'*Encyclopédie de l'Islam,* pourtant peu prolixe en la matière), de récits de voyage, de notes et de chroniques éparses dans de nombreux périodiques, qu'il est hors de question de citer ici. On se bornera donc ci-dessous aux études intéressant plus spécialement notre sujet ou envisageant les problèmes islamiques dans un cadre géographique déterminé. Telle qu'elle est, je pense que cette liste assez longue pourra rendre service à des islamisants comme à des géographes en les mettant respectivement en contact avec des travaux d'origine différente. Pour cette même raison j'ai commenté quelque peu cette bibliographie.

ABRÉVIATIONS.—*A.G.: Annales de géographie; A.I.E.O.:*

* Reprinted verbatim from the French edition of 1957 with the exception of a few changes made by the author.—PUB-LISHER'S NOTE

Annales de l'Institut d'Etudes orientales publiées par la Faculté des Lettres d'Alger; *Al. A.: Al Andalus. Revista de las escuelas de estudios arabes de Madrid y Granada; B.A.G.F.: Bulletin de l'Association de Géographes français; B.E.O.: Bulletin d'Etudes orientales* publié par l'Institut français de Damas; *D.E.O.: Documents . . . , ibid.; Hesp.: Hesperis; I.H.E.M.: Publications de l'Institut des Hautes Etudes marocaines; M.W.: The Moslem World; R.E.I.: Revue des Etudes islamiques; R.M.M.: Revue du monde musulman; S.I.: Studia islamica.*

Aspects d'ensemble

Célerier (J.), Islam et géographie, *Hesp.*, 1952, 3–4, pp. 331–371 (inégal, mais intéressant). Fleure, The geographical distribution of the major religions, *Bull. Soc. Roy. de Géog. d'Egypte*, t. XXIV, nov. 1951, pp. 1–18 (très court sur l'Islam mais quelques idées capitales). Gautier (E.-F.), *Mœurs et coutumes des Musulmans*, Paris, 1931 (brillant mais parfois dangereux). Gaudefroy-Demombynes, *Les institutions musulmanes*, 3ᵉ éd., Paris, 1946, chap. XII: «La vie économique», pp. 181–196. Géopolitique de l'Islam dans Bowman (I.), *The Mohammedan world*, New York, 1924.

Répartition générale des musulmans

La carte d'ensemble la plus récente est celle éditée par le Centre des Hautes Etudes d'Administration musulmane: *Les Musulmans dans le monde*, Paris, 1952, Editions de la Présidence du Conseil, avec notice de 42 p. (*La documentation française*, nᵒ 1642, 9 oct. 1952.) Remarquable réussite typographique en 7 couleurs, mais parfois insuffisante (admet sans discussion la «taqiyya» (hypocrisie) des chiites dans de nombreux cas, ce qui aboutit à les éliminer d'Anatolie et des Balkans). Ne dispense pas de recourir aux *Annuaires du monde musulman,* édités par L. MASSIGNON (le dernier, 4ᵉ éd., Paris, 1955, avec précieuses mises au point bibliographiques), ainsi qu'aux cartes détaillées par régions publiées dans la *R.M.M.* de 1923, t. LV, sous le titre «Le domaine de l'Islam». Voir encore LE CHATELIER (A.), Politique musulmane, *R.M.M.*, t. XII, 1910, I: Le monde musulman, pp. 5–48 (cartes).

L'ISLAM ET LA CITÉ

C'est de loin l'aspect qui a le plus retenu l'attention, tant des géographes que des historiens et orientalistes. Bibliographie déjà abondante et qui compte des œuvres maîtresses. GÉNÉRALITÉS.—MARÇAIS (W.), L'islamisme et la vie urbaine. *C.R. Ac. Inscrip.*, Paris, 1928, pp. 86–100. MARÇAIS (G.), L'urbanisme musulman, *Vᵉ Congrès de la Fédération des Soc. savantes d'Af. du N.*, Alger, 1940, pp. 13–34.— La conception des villes dans l'Islam, *Revue d'Alger*, II, 1945, pp. 517–533. BRUNSCHVIG (R.), Urbanisme médiéval et droit musulman, *R.E.I.*, 1947, pp. 127–155. PAUTY (Ed.), Villes spontanées et villes crées en Islam, *A.I.E.O.*, IX, 1951, pp. 52–75. GRUNEBAUM (G. E. VON), The Muslim town and the hellenistic town, *Scientia*, 1955, pp. 364–70.—Die islamische Stadt, *Saeculum*, VI, 2, 1955, pp. 138–153. CAHEN (C.), Zur Geschichte der staedtischen Gesellschaft im islamischen Orient des Mittelalters, *Saeculum*, IX, 1958, pp. 59–76. GOITEIN (S. D.), The Rise of the Near-Eastern Bourgeoisie in Early Islamic Times, *Journal of World History*, III, 1957, pp. 583–604. ETUDES DE CARACTÈRE RÉGIONAL ET PRINCIPALES MONOGRAPHIES.—Sur les villes hispano-musulmanes, nombreuses études de TORRES-BALBAS (L.). On citera: Les villes musulmanes d'Espagne et leur urbanisation, *A.I.E.O.*, VI, 1942–47, pp. 5–30.—Plazas, zocos y tiendas en las ciudades hispano-musulmanes, *Al. A.*, XII, 1947, pp. 437–441.—Estructura de las ciudades h.m.: la medina, los arrabales y los barrios, *Al. A.*, XVIII, 1953, pp. 149–177.—Extension y demografia de las ciudades h.m. *S.I.*, III, 1955, pp. 35–60. Sur les pays arabes: Passarge (S.), Stadtlandschaften im Arabischen Orient, in *Stadtlandschaften der Erde*, Hambourg, 1930. Despois (J.), *L'Afrique du Nord*, Paris, 1949, pp. 346 ss.—Kairouan, *A.G.*, 1930, pp. 159–177. Marçais (G.), Note sur les Ribats en Berbérie, *Mélanges Basset*, Paris, 1925, t. II, pp. 395–431. Lespes (R.), *Alger*, Paris, 1930. Mercier, *La civilisation urbaine au Mzab*, Paris, 1924. Massignon (L.), Enquête sur les corporations musulmanes d'artisans et de commerçants au Maroc, *R.M.M.*, LVIII, 1924, 2ᵉ section. Caille (J.), *La ville de Rabat jusqu'au protectorat français*, *I.H. Et. M.*, XLIV, 3 vol., Paris, 1949. Le Tourneau (R.), *Fès avant le protectorat*, *I.H. Et. M.*, XLV, Casablanca, 1949.—L'évolution des villes musulmanes d'Af. du N. au contact de l'Occident, *A.I.E.O.*, XII, 1954, pp. 199–222. Clerget (M.), De quelques caractères communs et distinctifs des villes arabes dans l'Orient médiéval, *Cong. int. de Géog.*, Paris, 1931, t. III, pp. 438–444.—*Le Caire, étude de géographie urbaine et d'histoire économique*, 2 vol., Le Caire, 1934. Boucheman (A. de), Une petite cité caravanière, Soukhne, *D.E.O.*, 1939, pp. 16–85. Weulersse (J.), Antioche, essai de géographie urbaine, *B.E.O.*, IV, 1934, pp. 27–79.—Antioche, un type de cité d'Islam. *Cong. int. de Géog.*, Varsovie, 1937, III, pp. 255–262.—La primauté des cités dans l'économie syrienne. *Cong. int. de Géog.*, Amsterdam, 1938, t. II, sect. 3 A, pp. 233–239.—Damas, étude de développement urbain, *B.A.G.F.*, 1936, pp. 5–9. Sauvaget (J.), *Alep*, Paris, 1941. Gautier (E.-F.), Les villes saintes de l'Arabie, *A.G.*, 1918, pp. 115–131. (Voir également sur Djeddah Rathjens (C.) et Wissmann (H. von), Landschaftskundliche Beobachtungen im südlichen Hedjaz: 4. Die Stadt Djeddah, *Erdkunde*, 1947.) Sur les villes turques: Busch-Zantner (R.), Zur Kenntnis der Osmanischen Stadt, *Geographische Zeitschrift*, 1932, pp. 1–13. Bartsch (G.), Stadtgeographische Probleme in Anatolien, *Deutschen Geographentag, Frankfurt, 1951*, Remagen, 1952, pp. 129–132.—Das Gebiet des Erciyes dagi und die Stadt Kayseri in Mittel Anatolien, *Jahrbuch d. Geog. Gesellschaft*, Hannover, 1934–35.—Ankara im Wandel der Zeiten und Kulturen, *Petermanns Mitteilungen*, 1954, pp. 256–266. Ergin (O.), *Istanbulda imar ve iskan hareketleri (Evolution de la construction et de l'habitat à Istanbul)*, Istanbul, 1938. Wilhelmy (H.), HochBulgarien II. Sofia: Wandlungen einer Grosstadt zwischen Orient und Occident, *Schriften d. Geog. Instituts der Universitat Kiel*, Band V, Heft 3, Kiel, 1936. Sur les villes persanes: Stratil-Sauer (G.), *Meschcd*, Leipzig, 1937.—Birdjand, eine ostpersische Stadt, *Mitteilungen d. Geog. Gesellschaft Wien*, Bd. 92, 1950, pp. 106–122. Sur les villes musulmanes de l'Inde voir la monographie de Qadiyan, ville sainte des Ahmadiyahs, dans Spate, *India and Pakistan*, London, 1954, pp. 189–192, et des éléments de comparaison entre villes musulmanes et indhouistes des plaines du Gange dans un article du même: Five cities of the Gangetic Plain, *Geographical review*, 1950, pp. 260–278. Sur la transformation des villes du Turkestan, voir Krafft (H.), *A travers le Turkestan russe*, Paris, 1902, chap. I: «Nouvelles villes russes» et II «Vieilles villes indigènes».

L'Islam et la maison urbaine.—Outre les monographies des diverses cités, qui contiennent souvent des paragraphes consacrés aux demeures privées, on citera: Marçais (G.), *Manuel d'art musulman. L'architecture (Islam occidental)*, 2 vol., Paris, 1926, (t. II, pp. 556 ss., 717 ss., 802 ss.).—Salle, antisalle. Recherches sur l'évolution d'un thème de l'architecture domestique en pays d'Islam, *A.I.E.O.*, X, 1952, pp. 274–301. Gallotti, *Le jardin et la maison arabe au Maroc*, 2 vol.,

Paris, 1926. GABRIEL (A.), *Les fouilles d'Al Foustat et les origines de la maison arabe en Egypte*, Paris, 1921. HULST (D') et PHÈNE SPIERS, The arab houses of Egypt. *Transactions of the Roy. Inst. of British Architect.*, VI, Londres, 1880. PAUTY (E.), *Palais et maisons d'époque musulmane au Caire*, Le Caire, 1933. CLERGET (M.), L'habitation indigène au Caire, *A.G.*, 1931, pp. 527–541. THOUMIN (R.), La maison syrienne, *D.E.O.*, II, Paris, 1932. REUTHER, *Das Wohnhaus in Bagdad und anderen Staedten des Irak*, Berlin, 1910. KÖMÜR-CÜOGLU (E.), *Ankara evleri* (*Les maisons d'Ankara*), Istanbul, 1950.

L'ISLAM ET L'EXPLOITATION DU SOL

L'ATTITUDE DE L'ISLAM A L'ÉGARD DE LA TERRE est bien caractérisée par J. WEULERSSE, *Paysans de Syrie et du Proche-Orient*, Paris, 1946, pp. 66 ss. Un texte capital pour les conceptions agraires de l'Islam est celui de EL-BOUKHARI, *Livres de l'ensemencement et de la mousâqât*, trad. PELTIER, Alger, 1949 (avec précieux commentaires du traducteur). Pour les interminables discussions sur la légitimité des contrats de métayage on pourra voir par exemple ABOU YOU-SOUF YAKOUB, *Le livre de l'impôt foncier*, trad. FAGNAN, Paris, 1921. Les tentatives des théologiens modernes pour exposer les encouragements de l'Islam à l'agriculture restent bien ternes. Voir par exemple MAHMUD AHMAD, *Economics of Islam*, Lahore, 1947, pp. 160 ss.

En ce qui concerne LE PROBLÈME FONCIER en pays musulman, la bibliographie est considérable. Une bonne liste récente des sources et études générales sur le régime foncier islamique pourra être cherchée dans LAMBTON (A. K. S.), *Landlord and peasant in Persia*, Oxford, 1953. Pour une rapide initiation on se reportera encore aux études classiques de BELIN, Etudes sur la propriété foncière en pays musulmans et spécialement en Turquie, *Journal asiatique*, 1861–62, et même de Worms, Recherches sur la constitution de la propriété territoriale dans les pays musulmans, *Journal asiatique*, 1842–44. Pour le caractère pré-islamique de la tendance à l'étatisation du sol chez les Turcs voir Turan (O.), Türkiye selcuklularinda toprak hukuku (Le droit foncier chez les Seldjoukides de Turquie), *Belleten*, 1948, n° 47, pp. 549–574 (et *R.E.I.*, 1948). Discussion du même problème dans Cahen (Cl.), Le régime de la terre et l'occupation turque en Anatolie, *Cahiers d'Histoire mondiale*, II, 3, 1955, pp. 566–580. Pour l'influence du droit musulman sur les pays balkaniques, voir Barkan (O. L.), Aperçu sur l'histoire des problèmes agraires des pays balkaniques, *Rev. Fac. Sc. Econ. de l'Univ. d'Istanbul*, 1945–46, n°s 1–4, pp. 120–172. Excellente étude d'un exemple régional dans Despois (J.), *La Tunisie orientale, Sahel et basse steppe*, Paris, 1940, IVe Partie, chap. I: «Le problème foncier», pp. 321–349. Enfin les conséquences du régime foncier islamique n'ont, à notre connaissance, pas été plus brillamment exposées que dans une thèse de l'Université de Berne: Gurland (A.), *Grundzüge des muhammedanischen Agrarverfassung und Agrarpolitik*, Dorpat, 1907.

L'Islam et les interdits.—Sur la vigne: Isnard (H.), *La vigne en Algérie* (liv. II, chap. II: «La viticulture dans l'Algérie musulmane»), pp. 261–273, Gap, 1947. Lefebvre (Th.), La vigne en Turquie, *A.G.*, 1930, pp. 186–190. Sur les difficultés de la viticulture chypriote sous le régime musulman, cf. Baker, *Cyprus as I saw it in 1879*, London, 1879, chap. X: «The wine district of Limasol», pp. 267–292. Sur la consommation de l'alcool dans un pays musulman, Tumertekin (E.), Tûrkiyede içki istihlâkinin cografi dagilisi (The geographical distribution of the consumption of alcoholic beverages in Turkey), *Rev. of the geog. inst. of the univ. of Istanbul,* t. I, n° 2, 1951, pp. 70–81, avec résumé anglais.

Sur l'Islam et le porc, aucune étude d'ensemble, cf. Marty (P.), Les Nimadi, Maures sauvages et chasseurs, *Hesp.*, 1930, pp. 119–124. Sur la cynophagie dans l'Islam, longue note critique et bibliographique de Canard (M.), L'autobiographie d'un chambellan . . . , Note infrapaginale, pp. 298–99, *Hesp.*, 1952.

Les apports de l'Islam a l'exploitation du sol.—Sur l'olivier, Clermont-Ganneau, La lampe et l'olivier dans le Coran, *Rev. de l'Hist. des Religions*, 1920, pp. 213–259. Sur l'Islam et la vie rurale et pastorale en Afrique Noire, nombreuses remarques éparses dans l'œuvre de P. Marty (voir plus loin). Sur l'apport de l'Islam aux techniques d'irrigation mise au point de Torres-Balbas (L.), Las norias fluviales en España, *Al. A.*, V, 1940, pp. 195–208. Sur l'origine préislamique des coutumiers d'irrigation du Proche-Orient, cf. Tresse (R.), L'irrigation dans la Ghouta de Damas, *R.E.I.*, 1929, pp. 459–573.

Enfin quantité de données concernant la matière du chapitre I, B, sont à chercher dans les études régionales énumérées plus loin.

Pèlerinages islamiques

Pèlerinage de La Mecque: Tresse (R.), *Le pèlerinage syrien aux villes saintes de l'Islam*, Paris, 1937. Duguet, *Le pèlerinage de La Mecque*, Paris, 1932. Rathjens, *Die Pilgerfahrt nach Mekka*, Hamburg, 1948. Stanton et Pickens, The Mecca pilgrimage, *M.W.*, 1934, pp. 229–235.

Sur la complexité de la répartition géographique des pèlerinages dans l'Islam on pourra se faire une idée dans Dermenghem (E.), *Le culte des saints dans l'Islam maghrébin,* Paris, 1954 (bibliographie, p. 180). Canaan (T.), *Mo-*

hammedan saints and sanctuaries in Palestine, London, 1925. HASLUCK (F. W.), *Christianity and Islam under the sultans*, 2 vol., Oxford, 1929, t. I, Part. I (pour le substrat préislamique dans les pèlerinages musulmans).

GENRES DE VIE RELIGIEUX EN PAYS D'ISLAM

Il y a fort peu à tirer de la littérature sur les confréries, dont la base n'est généralement pas géographique. Cf. à ce sujet, MICHAUX-BELLAIRE, Essai sur l'histoire des confréries marocaines, *Hesp.*, 1921, pp. 141–159. DERMENGHEM, *op. cit.* Pour les exceptions, BARKAN (O. L.), Les derviches colonisateurs turcs de l'époque de la conquête et la zaviye, *Vakiflar dergisi* (*Revue des wakfs*), t. II, Ankara, 1942, pp. 279–386. HERBER (J.), Les Hamadcha et les Dghoughiyyin, *Hesp.*, 1923, pp. 217–235. Sur les tribus maraboutiques, études de Marty sur la Mauritanie citées plus loin. CHAUMEIL (J.), Histoire d'une tribu maraboutique de l'Anti-Atlas: les Ait Abdallah ou Said, *Hesp.*, 1952, pp. 197–212.

SÉGRÉGATIONS D'ORIGINE HÉRÉTIQUE ET MINORITAIRE

Indispensable vue générale sur le critère de l'hérésie en pays d'Islam (subversion politique et refus de l'ordre existant) dans LEWIS (B.), Some observations on the significance of heresy in the history of Islam, *S.I.*, I, 1953, pp. 43–63. On citera ci-dessous les principaux travaux comportant des études détaillées sur la répartition géographique et des renseignements sur le genre de vie.

Sur le Kharedjisme, voir GAUTIER (E.-F.), *Les siècles obscurs du Maghreb*, Paris, 1927. DESPOIS (J.), *Le Djebel Nefousa*, Paris, 1935. MERCIER, *op. cit.* Sur les Zkaras, MOULIERAS, Les Zkaras, une tribu zénète anti-musulmane au Maroc, *Bull. de la Soc. de Géog. d'Oran*, 1903–1905. Pour les Mourides, ouvrage cité plus loin de GOUILLY et MARTY

(P.), Les Mourides du Sénégal, *R.M.M.*, t. XXV, 1913, pp. 1–164. Pour les Ghoudf, bibliographie dans DERMENGHEM, *op. cit.*, p. 241.

Sur le Proche-Orient en général, WEULERSSE, *Paysans de Syrie . . .* , pp. 71–79. Données numériques dans HOURANI (A. H.), *Minorities in the arab world*, Oxford, 1947. VAUMAS (E. DE), La répartition confessionnelle au Liban et l'équilibre de l'Etat libanais, *Rev. de Géog. alpine*, 1955, pp. 511–604 (avec carte h.-t. de la répartition des différentes confessions). WEULERSSE (J.), Problèmes d'Irak, *A.G.*, 1934, pp. 49–75, spécialement pp. 70–75 (avec carte). A compléter pour les Mandéens du bas Irak par DROWER, *The Mandeans of Irak and Iran*, Oxford, 1937. Sur les Nosaïris, WEULERSSE (J.), *Le pays des Alaouites*, Tours, 1940. THOUMIN, *Le Ghab*, Grenoble, 1936. Sur les Ismaéliens, LEWIS (N. N.), The Ismailis of Syria to-day, *Journal of the Royal Central Asian Society*, t. XXXIX, 1952, pp. 69–77. BOBRINSKOI (A.), La secte des Ismaéliens dans les possessions russes et boukhariennes de l'Asie centrale, *Etnograf. Obozr. (Rev. ethnographique)*, 1902, nº 2 (en russe). Sur les Druzes BEN-ZVI (I.), The Druze community in Israel, *Israel exploration journal*, 1954, nº 2, pp. 65–76. Sur les Yezidis, GUÉRINOT (A.), Les Yezidis, *R.M.M.*, t. V, 1908, pp. 581–630. LESCOT, *Enquête sur les Yezidis de Syrie et du Djebel Sindjar*, Beyrouth, 1938 (cartes). DAMLOOJI (S.), *The Yezidis*, 1949. Sur les Guèbres HOUTUM-SCHINDLER, Die Parsen in Persien, ihre Sprache und einige ihrer Gebräuche, *Zeit, d. Deutsch Morgenland. Gesellschaft*, 1882, t. XXXIV, p. 54. MENANT (D.), Les Zoroastriens de Perse, *R.M.M.T.*, III, 1907, pp. 193–220 et 421–452. Sur les Alévites d'Anatolie et de Perse, MINORSKY, *Notes sur la secte des Ahl-i-Hakk*, Paris, 1922 (et *R.M.M.*), avec carte. BIRGE (J. K.), *The Bektashi order of dervishes*, London, 1937. HASLUCK (F. W.), *op. cit.*, t. II,

chap. XLII: «Geographical distribution of the Bektashi.»
Plus particulièrement sur les Tahtadjis, Yusuf Ziya, *Anadolu
alevileri ve tahtacilari* (Les Alévites et Tahtadjis d'Anatolie),
Ilahiyat fakültesi mecmuasi (*Rev. de la Fac. de Théologie*),
Istanbul, 1928–29. Petersen (E.) et Luschan (F. von),
Reisen in Lykien, Milyas und Kibyratis, Wien, 1889, chap.
XIII: «Anthropologische Studien», A) Die Tachtadschy und
andere überreste der alten Bevölkerung, pp. 198–213. Yeti-
sen (R.), Naldöken Tahtacilari (Les Tahtadjis de Naldöken), *Türk foklor arastirmalari* (*Recherches folkloriques
turques*), nᵒˢ 17–55, 1950–54.

Bonnes remarques générales sur l'évolution du judaïsme
rural dans Chaumeil (J.), Le mellah de Tahala au pays des
Ammeln, *Hesp.*, 1953, pp. 227–240. Voir également Slousch
(N.), Les Jiufs de Debdou, *R.M.M.*, 1913, t. XXII, pp. 221–
69.

Études régionales et limites de l'Islam

Le problème des facteurs géographiques de l'expansion de
l'Islam n'a été étudié qu'exceptionnellement en lui-même. On
citera ci-dessous, outre les études donnant des renseignements
statistiques détaillés, les principaux ouvrages étudiant les
problèmes islamiques dans des cadres régionaux déterminés,
et qui peuvent aider à une approche du problème, en même
temps qu'ils fournissent des données sur la marque géographique de l'Islam. On a exclu tout ce qui concerne la
diaspora islamique contemporaine (Islam américain, Nord-
Africain en France par exemple) qui reste par son caractère
contingent tout à fait en marge de notre propos.

Afrique Occidentale.—Nombreuses études françaises
d'ensemble sur l'islamisation de l'Afrique Noire. La plus
récente est celle de Gouilly (A.), *L'Islam dans l'A.O.F.*,
Paris, 1952 (Bibliographie). Pour les données sur la réparti-

tion des musulmans on pourra se reporter à Urvoy (Y.), *Petit atlas ethno-démographique du Soudan*, Paris, 1940 (carte IV). Lighton (C.), The numerical strength of Islam in the Soudan, *M.W.*, 1936, pp. 253–273, avec estimation critique de la cadence des progrès. Problème des limites abordé plus spécialement dans Azan (P.), Les limites de l'Islam africain. *L'Afrique et l'Asie*, II, Paris, 1948, pp. 16–30. Coppet (M. de), L'Islam et la forêt, *Résonances*, 1949, n° 3, pp. 17 ss. Brévie, *Islamisme contre «naturisme» au Soudan français*, Paris, 1923. Delafosse (M.), L'animisme nègre et sa résistance à l'islamisation en Afrique Occidentale, *R.M.M.*, t. XLIX, 1921, pp. 121–164 (carte). Pour les causes de la résistance mossi voir Gautier (E.-F.), *L'Afrique Noire occidentale*, Paris, 1943, pp. 131 ss., et Urvoy, *Atlas* . . . , p. 14. Sur les Bambaras Monteil (C.), *Les Bambaras*, Paris, 1924, chap. VI: «L'Islam en pays bambara». Les études déjà anciennes de Marty (P.) sont une mine irremplaçable de renseignements de détail: *L'Islam en Mauritanie et au Sénégal*, Paris, 1915–16; *L'Islam au Sénégal*, 2 vol., Paris, 1917; *L'Islam et les tribus maures: les Brakna*, Paris, 1921; *L'Islam en Guinée*, Paris, 1921; *L'Islam en Côte d'Ivoire*, Paris, 1922; *L'Islam et les tribus du Soudan*, 4 vol., Paris, 1918–22; *L'Islam au Dahomey*, Paris, 1926.

Afrique Centrale, Orientale et Sud-Orientale.—Ancieux, *Le problème musulman dans l'Afrique belge*, Institut royal colonial belge, Mémoires in-8° de la Sect. des Sc. morales et polit., t. XVIII, 1949. Trimingham, *Islam in the Sudan*, Oxford, 1949.—*Islam in Ethiopia*, London, 1952. Zwemer (S. M.), Islam in Ethiopia and Eritrea, *M.W.*, t. XXVI, 1936, pp. 5–15. Guérinot (A.), L'Islam en Abyssinie, *R.M.M.*, t. XXXIV, 1916, pp. 1–66. Ferrand (G.), *Les Musulmans à Madagascar et aux Comores*, 3 vol., Paris, 1891–1902. Zwemer (S. M.), Islam in Madagascar, *M.W.*, 1940, pp. 151–167. GASSITA, L'Islam à l'île Maurice, *R.M.M.*, 1912, t. XXI. KLAMROTH, *Der Islam in Deutsch OstAfrika*, Berlin, 1912. HAGEL (F.), Der Islam in SüdAfrika, *Neue Zeitschrift für Missionswissenschaft*, Heft I, 1952, pp. 28–36. DU PLESSIS, Muslims in South Africa, *Islamic Review*, mars 1952, pp. 17–19.

ASIE: Généralités: ROUX (J. P.), *L'Islam en Asie*, Paris, 1958. Indonésie et Pacifique.—BOUSQUET, Introduction à l'étude de l'Islam indonésien, *R.E.I.*, 1938. ROBEQUAIN (C.), *Le monde malais*, Paris, 1946, pp. 86–90. BERG (C. C.), The islamisation of Java, *S.I.*, IV, 1955, pp. 111–142. HUNT (C. L.), Moslem and Christian in the Philippines, *Pacific Affairs*, 1955, pp. 331–349. DJINGUIZ (M.), L'Islam en Australie et en Polynésie, *R.M.M.*, t. IV, 1908, pp. 75–85.

Indochine.—CABATON (A.), Notes sur l'Islam dans l'Indochine française, *R.M.M.*, t. I, 1906–07, pp. 27–47.—Les Chams musulmans dans l'Indochine française, *R.M.M.*, t. II, 1907, pp. 129–180. NER (M.), Les Musulmans de l'Indochine française, *Bull. Ecole franç. d'Extrême-Orient*, Hanoï, 1941, t. XLI, fasc. 2 (carte). RONDOT (P.), Notes sur les Chams Bani du Binh Thuan, *R.E.I.*, 1949, pp. 13–47 (carte).

Inde.—Aucune bonne étude d'ensemble sur l'Islam indien. VINSON (J.), Les musulmans du Sud de l'Inde, *R.M.M.*, t. II, 1907, pp. 199–204 et t. XIII, 1911, pp. 95–108. BOUVAT (L.), Les Moplahs du Sud de l'Inde, *R.M.M.*, t. XLVII, 1921, pp. 65–92. MENANT (D.), Les Khodjas du Guzarate, *R.M.M.*, t. X, 1910, pp. 214–32 et 406–24.—Les Bohoras du Guzarate, *R.M.M.*, t. X, 1910, pp. 465–493. Carte de la répartition des Musulmans (avant la partition) dans DAVIS (K.), *The population of India and Pakistan*, Princeton, 1951, p. 197.

Chine.—BROOMHALL (M.), *Islam in China*, London, 1910. Mission D'OLLONE, *Recherches sur les Musulmans chinois*, Paris, 1911. SOULIÉ (G.), Les Musulmans du Yunnan,

R.M.M., t. IX, 1909, pp. 209–23. Cordier (G.), Les Musulmans du Yunnan, *R.M.M.*, t. XXIV, 1913, pp. 318–26. Contento (P. A.), Islam in Yunnan to-day, *M.W.*, t. XXX, 1940.

Asie centrale.—Griebenow (M. G.), Islam in Tibet, *M.W.*, 1936, pp. 127–29. Les conditions de l'islamisation sont le mieux dégagées dans Barthold, *Histoire des Turcs d'Asie centrale*, trad. fr., Paris, 1945, chap. III et IV.

U.R.S.S.—Bobrovnikoff (Mme), The Moslems in Russia, *M.W.*, 1911 (cartes). Castagne (J.), Russie slave et Russie turque, *R.M.M.*, t. LVI, 1923. II: *Etude géographique des éléments islamisés*, pp. 12–92.

Europe: Balkans.—Balagija (A.), *Les Musulmans yougoslaves*, Alger, 1940. Hangi (A.), *Die Moslim's in Bosnien-Hercegovina, ihre Lebensweise, Sitten und Gebraüche*, Sarajevo, 1907. Sur les conditions de l'islamisation, Barkan (O.-L.), Les déportations comme méthode de peuplement et de colonisation dans l'empire ottoman, *Rev. Fac. Sc. Econ. Univ. d'Istanbul*, t. XI, 1949–50, fasc. 1–4, pp. 67–131, donne une carte indiquant la répartition géographique des populations par confession dans les pays balkaniques au début du xvie siècle.

Méditerranée occidentale.—On doit se borner à des ouvrages historiques généraux: Levi-Provençal, *L'Espagne musulmane au Xe siècle*, Paris, 1932, et les trois premiers tomes (seuls parus) de l'*Histoire de l'Espagne musulmane* du même auteur. Amari (M.), *Storia dei Musulmani di Sicilia*, Catana, 5 vol., 1933–39. Davin, *Les esclaves sarrasins en Provence*, Toulon, 1943.